The art of being you

"A collection of essays for self-growth and self-discovery"

Amy Reis Williams

© Copyright 2020 - All rights reserved.

The content contained within this book may not be reproduced, duplicated or transmitted without direct written permission from the author or the publisher.

Under no circumstances will any blame or legal responsibility be held against the publisher, or author, for any damages, reparation, or monetary loss due to the information contained within this book, either directly or indirectly.

Legal Notice:

This book is copyright protected. It is only for personal use. You cannot amend, distribute, sell, use, quote or paraphrase any part, or the content within this book, without the consent of the author or publisher.

Disclaimer Notice:

Please note the information contained within this document is for educational and entertainment purposes only. All effort has been executed to present accurate, up to date, reliable, complete information. No warranties of any kind are declared or implied. Readers acknowledge that the author is not engaged in the rendering of legal, financial, medical or professional advice. The content within this book has been derived from various sources.

Please consult a licensed professional before attempting any techniques outlined in this book.

By reading this document, the reader agrees that under no circumstances is the author responsible for any losses, direct or indirect, that are incurred as a result of the use of the information contained within this document, including, but not limited to, errors, omissions, or inaccuracies.

DEDICATION

This book is dedicated to my children for whatever life throws at you. Remember to never let it dull your light because you are amazing, fearless and resilient. To anyone who has ever felt lost, hurt and unsure of themselves. To anyone who has suffered mental illness or ever felt alone—you are not. We all share feelings and have had difficulties in some shape or form, even if they are never spoken about; we have all been there.

Table of Contents

INTRODUCTION 1

CHAPTER 1: GROW 5

The Wonderful Ways You'll Change by Putting Yourself First .8
Ways to Accept Yourself for Who You Are 10
Develop a Relationship With Your Highest Self 14
The Growth of Your Self-Esteem 16
Reasons to Listen to Your Intuition....................................... 19
The Power of Positive Thinking: Mindful Habits for Creating a Positive Life... 21
Self-Care Tips That Are Tough but Life-Changing 24
To the Highly Sensitive and the Empath: You're Abilities Are a Blessing 27
Learn How to Fall Forward.. 29
Realise Your Full Potential by Conquering Your Fears 31
Your Pain Can Help You Grow... 34
25 Reminders You Are Enough 36

CHAPTER 2: RIPPLES..51

The Ripples of Psychological Trauma and Its Effects 54
When You Fail, Fall Forward... 56
How You Can Master Your Reactions to Stress..................... 58
25 Affirmations to Begin Your Day With Positive Ripples...... 62
Signs You Might Be in an Emotionally Abusive Relationship... 65
Ways to Turn a Bad Day into a Good Day 69
Small Ways to Practise Self-Care When You Feel Too Busy ... 72
Benefits of Getting a Good Night's Sleep.............................. 74
Overcoming Your Fears: Facing Anxiety and Phobias............ 76

CHAPTER 3: AWARENESS 81

The Five Stages of Awareness Mastery 82

The Levels of Self-Awareness 86
Importance of Mindfulness 88
Awareness of Your Mental Health 89
Reaching Your Emotional Intelligence 91
Signs Your Self-Confidence is Low and How to Start Loving Yourself 92
It's Time to Stop Doubting Yourself 96
Benefits That Prove It's Good to Cry 99
Tips to Help You Manage a Healthier Eating Lifestyle 101

CHAPTER 4: BREATHE 108

Don't Rush Through Your Life, Notice the Beauty 110
It's Better to Breathe Than to Plan 112
Important Steps of Mindfulness Meditation 114
Always Remember to Breathe 116
Release Yourself From Past Hurt and Trauma 118
Here Are 10 Reminders to Help You When You're Struggling to Better Yourself 121
Ways to Help You Cope With Anxiety Right Now 124
Help Yourself Heal From a Narcissistic Relationship 127

CHAPTER 5: GRATITUDE 133

Be Grateful for Your Failures 134
Benefits of Gratitude for Everlasting Peace and Happiness .. 137
Simple Ways to Practise Gratitude 141
You Are Never Alone 144
Tips for Keeping a Gratitude Journal 145
Why You Should Be Thankful for What You Don't Have 148
A Dozen Ways to Love Your Body 150
A 30-Day Gratitude Challenge 152

CONCLUSION 159

REFERENCES 161

Introduction

"Letting go of past wounds and not worrying about the future are two of the most difficult tasks a person can undertake, but reminding ourselves that it is our present that needs our attention can be the key to real peace"- Amy Reis Williams

You are unique. There is no one in this world like you. This is why it's important to be you.

The struggle you might have is the same story for many of us—you question who you are. You question your belief, abilities, and your life's mission. You ask yourself, "Am I doing this right?" "Why am I here?" "What is the point of this situation?" and "Is there something different, something better, that I should be doing?"

Sometimes you feel that you're lost in the crowd. You know you're supposed to stand out, but you don't know how. You might be afraid. You might feel that you don't deserve the light shining on you. You might have a burning feeling deep inside you that wants to escape, but you don't know how to free it. You don't know what steps to take to truly be you.

This book is here to help you shine. I've written it for you so you can learn to connect with your highest self and reach your life's mission. It will help you become more self-aware and comfortable in your own skin.

There are over 50 essays that focus on ways you can improve your life and learn more about yourself. You'll discover the power of positive thinking, how you can fall forward, develop a relationship with your highest self, and manage your reaction to stress. You'll learn the importance of putting yourself first, taking that precious "me time," and how to overcome the feeling of guilt. Let gratitude teach you how to become thankful for your failures and reach your happiness. You will feel the power of meditation and how to develop your self-esteem.

These essays are for the person who is struggling with their self-confidence, afraid to step out of their comfort zone because they don't know their potential. If you're working on learning more about yourself so you can achieve your dreams, this book is for you. It's for the person who feels lost, like they don't belong, who's told they're too sensitive, or for those who are trying to reach their highest self. It's for the human being interested in self-growth and self-discovery. It's for you, the one who is reading this now and wondering if you have the power to overcome your negative mindset.

Read these essays one-by-one and incorporate them into your life. You don't need to read them in order. In fact, you can decide to pick an essay every day and work on reaching your highest self in small steps. Some will be harder than others, but don't give up. You can achieve anything you set your mind to. You're a strong and resilient person. You're powerful.

"Our Brain is a powerful machine arguably the most powerful machine ever created, it's super complex and totally organic."
- Amy Reis Williams

Chapter 1:

Grow

"Every moment of one's existence, one is growing into more or retreating into less." —Norman Mailer ("15 Personal Development Quotes," 2017).

Personal development is a lifelong process. You don't always realise that you're internally growing because it's a natural process of life. Other times you strive for change and work hard to improve a piece of your personality. You might aim for higher self-compassion or to become more patient with people. You use self-growth to access your skills so you can develop goals.

There are several components of growth but one of the most important is Abraham Maslow's Hierarchy of Needs, a motivational theory developed in 1943 (Mcleod, 2020). The original model is usually shown in a pyramid and consists of five models. At the bottom you have your two basic needs. The first is physiological, such as water, rest, food, and warmth. Moving up the pyramid, you find your safety needs, such as the feeling of security. Next, you have your two psychological needs. The first one and third model in the pyramid is the need for love and belonging. The next focuses on esteem and your need to feel accomplished. At the top of the pyramid is your self-fulfilment needs, also known as self-actualisation. These include achieving your full potential, reaching your highest self, and creativity.

There is a modern version of the Hierarchy of Needs which include several areas separated into two basic needs: deficiency and growth. Deficiency needs are at the bottom of the pyramid and focus on four needs, which are physiological, safety, belonging, and esteem. The rest of the pyramid holds the four growth needs starting with cognitive and moving up to aesthetic, self-actualisation, and transcendence.

Once you understand the Hierarchy of Needs you can start to grow. You can learn how to connect with your highest self, manage your personal development, establish SMART goals, declutter your mind and environment, learn about its five stages, and continue to emotionally and psychologically grow.

The Wonderful Ways You'll Change by Putting Yourself First

It's not easy to put yourself first, especially if you have a family to think about. You always want to ensure you do everything you can to make your children and partner happy. You need to be there to take care of your parents as they grow older. You want to help your boss succeed and see the company grow. You find yourself taking time to volunteer at a homeless shelter because you feel the need to give back. By the time you go to bed, you're too exhausted to think about yourself, so you go to bed and start your day focusing on other people all over again.

While putting other people first is a great quality, you can dig yourself into an emotional dark hole; one you can find yourself struggling to crawl out of when you realise you need to take time for yourself.

The biggest problem when you put others first is that your emotional and mental health starts to decline, which causes your physical health to fade. Thankfully, you can change your mindset to ensure that *you* come first, but you need to understand the ways you'll change to justify this action.

Your communication skills improve. You might not realise that when you're emotionally and mentally struggling your communication isn't as strong as it could be. This is mainly because you're not communicating with yourself. The way you talk to yourself can make a difference in how you view the world. When you hear what you're telling yourself, your listening ears develop. There is a clear difference between hearing and listening. When you hear the words go into your ears but not into your mind. When you listen, you process what is being said so you can analyse it and help. This means that when you start listening to yourself, you'll become more open to other people and help them efficiently, too.

You become happier. When you spend time with yourself you get to know you on a different level. Think about how much you know about your significant other or close friends because of the time you spend with them—the same goes for you. This helps you become happier because you learn what your heart truly desires. You discover how much you can accomplish, and you start to believe in yourself more. Another reason for the increase in happiness is because you start to control your stress and anxiety more. When you learn about yourself, you can focus on the areas in your life that need improvement and truly start to help yourself on a different level.

Your confidence increases. Your inner growth will start to show itself as confidence. You'll start to accomplish more than you imagined because you know what you're capable of. Furthermore, you will become less afraid to try something new because you understand that failure is a part of internal development. Knowing that you are enough puts a skip in your step, and you head toward increased self-esteem and confidence. You also begin to value yourself more, which improves your overall self-worth.

There are other positive changes that you'll make when you start to focus on yourself. You'll also begin to realise that taking time out for you doesn't mean you're ignoring other people. It doesn't make you a bad person, wife, mum, or employee—it makes you a better one.

Ways to Accept Yourself for Who You Are

You can put yourself first and feel the changes bubbling inside of you, but this doesn't mean that you're truly accepting yourself. It's often a challenging step because you need to learn how to adapt to difficult situations.

Take a moment to think about how accepting you are of other people. Do you generally stay away from judgement? Are people comfortable being themselves around you? Now, you need to look at how you accept yourself. If you're like many other people, you have trouble with this part because you know everything that's wrong with you. Your inner critical voice isn't shy. If you accept other people more than yourself, you're too hard on you.

No one is better than you. It doesn't matter if they can sing sweeter, paint prettier, or draw more sophisticated than you. We were all created equal when it comes to our unique set of talents and skills. You can achieve greatness just like anyone else.

When you accept yourself and start loving you for everything you can accomplish, you feel happier. You start to follow your path and fulfil your dreams and goals.

Learn to accept yourself just like you are by following these tips:

Focus on your positive qualities. You have more positive features than you realise at this moment. Grab a paper and pen and start writing down the ones that you know off the top of your head. Write down anything that comes to mind. For example, you're a good spouse, parent, sibling, child, student, cook, and employee. You're also compassionate, full of love, and want to see other people succeed. Text or call your friends and ask them what they believe your best quality is. Take time to write down as much as you can. You can even give yourself examples, such as you helped an elderly lady cross the street or you volunteer at a local non-profit.

Set the intention to accept yourself. Now that your mind is glowing with positivity, it's time to set the intention to accept yourself for who you are. When you do this, you'll start to shift your focus from blame, shame, and doubt to trust, acceptance, and tolerance. You will start to feel that you're leading a satisfying and happy life, and this will continue to solidify your mindset towards self-acceptance. The key is to tell yourself that you will make this your attention, similar to stating a goal. For example, you will look in the mirror and say, "Today I set my intention to accept everything about me, from the good to the bad. I will thrive in my strengths. I will accept my weaknesses and continue to work toward creating a fulfilling life."

Use positive self-talk. How often do you talk to yourself positively? How many times a day do you tell yourself "good job," or that you're proud of you? How often do you take part in negative self-talk? How many times a day do you say, "Why did I do this?" or "Did I really make that mistake?" Because your brain is wired to think about the bad before the good, it's more natural to engage in negative self-talk than the positive variety. But, it's also possible to change this thought process. The way you speak to yourself is your choice. Become mindful of your thoughts, and when you notice the negative creeping up, gently stop these thoughts and substitute the positives. You should take time out of your day, especially in the morning, to compliment yourself. You might say, "You look beautiful today," or "You're a rockstar and you're going to rock this day."

Grieve the loss of your unrealised dreams. It happens to everyone. No matter how hard you work, you don't always reach all of your goals. You can't take the holiday you've dreamed of for years and saved up for because you had a financial emergency or traveling is restricted. You never made it to the Olympics like you dreamed about as a child or you're heading toward a divorce when you imagined staying married forever. When you lose a dream, you need to grieve because it is a loss. It's just like losing someone you love because you loved that dream and you worked hard to try to make it a reality. You will find yourself going through the stages of grief—let it happen. Don't feel ashamed because it was only a wish or dream. It was a part of you, and now you feel like it's gone forever. Let yourself go through the stages, so you can accept the loss.

Realise you can never make everyone happy. No matter how hard you try, there will still be someone who doesn't like what you say or do. Accept it and move on. Don't worry about what other people think when it comes to your life because it's *your* life. You need to do what makes you happy and improves your quality of life. When it comes to making your own decisions, look at the priorities in your life and then come up with a plan. Furthermore, be confident with your decision and know that you made the right choice.

Try your best and accept that you did everything you could. Don't let your mind bring you back to the "what ifs." Once you go through a situation, tell yourself that you did your best. Tell yourself that you did everything you could in that moment and use any pieces of the experience as a way to develop yourself further. If you need to, find a way to forgive yourself. Move on from the situation with a commitment that you will try again and harder the next time.

Develop a Relationship With Your Highest Self

Have you ever had a conversation with your highest self? The person that you strive to become, the real you, the one who is so much more than what people see on the outside. Sometimes it's the part you hide from other people because you want to fit in with the crowd. Other times it's the person that helps you make smarter decisions and gives you motivation to reach your goals.

The key to reaching your full potential is to communicate with your highest self. You might go on a date or spend time hiking in nature. You might find that you communicate best when you write in your journal or paint a picture. The way you connect with your highest self depends on you. There is no right or wrong way.

When you connect with your highest self you reach your higher consciousness. This is the part of the human mind that is capable of reaching levels you never imagined.

You gain insight into your spiritual side and continue to become self-aware.

The trouble is, we spend most of our time in our lower consciousness, what some refer to as our reality. Naturally, you spend more time looking at the material world around you, what people think about you, and how you look. It's up to you to open the doorway to both of your conscious sides.

To communicate with your highest self, you need to open yourself up to your emotions. You need to follow your gut. You need to realise that there is more to the world than what you can see or touch. There's a whole other side, the waves of the universe, that help direct you down your right path so you can fulfil your life's mission.

Sometimes your higher self will be voices you hear in your head. Other times they're messages that urge you to do or not to do something.

Start connecting to your highest self by getting calm and centred. Visualise a place that makes you feel at peace; one full of natural beauty. This is a sacred place. It's where you go when you want to feel safe or need a break from the world around you.

Introduce yourself to your higher state of consciousness. Welcome the presence of your higher self into your sacred place. Now, ask yourself the first burning question that pops into your mind. Sit still and allow the answer to come to you. It might come as an emotion, voices, or by seeing words in your mind's eye.

Finally, write down what you heard, saw, or felt in your journal. Practise this exercise as much as possible. Open the doorway wide so you can get to know your highest self and grow internally.

The Growth of Your Self-Esteem

One of the most important pieces of you is your self-esteem. You want to ensure that you take care of yourself so you have a positive mindset that helps you believe in you, which will help your self-esteem blossom. It's important to understand that it's different from self-confidence. Your confidence focuses more on your skills, such playing sports, writing, or performing surgery. It can change depending on the situation and your knowledge. Your self-esteem is how you feel about yourself overall.

When you develop your self-esteem, you need to focus on your personal growth. You need to open up your mind and heart so you can start to believe in your abilities and what you can accomplish. There are many steps that you can follow to increase your self-esteem, but it's important to focus on only one or two at the same time.

If you start to overload yourself, you can take a few steps backwards instead of forward.

One step is to realise it's up to you to change your story. There is very little that you can truly control in your life. For example, you can't control the way someone else treats you or what they think about your work, but you can control how you react to their treatment. Keep in mind, your story runs deeper than what goes on in the physical world around you, it also includes the way you treat yourself. You are your worst critic so when you're telling yourself, "I'm being lazy" or "I'm not doing this right," you'll start to believe it. Therefore, you need to focus on positive thoughts like, "This project is a challenge, but with dedication and looking at different avenues I will accomplish it."

You can also focus on your strengths as a guide in developing your self-esteem. Think about it this way, everyone is good at something and not so good at something else. You need to find your inner rockstar and remember how confident you feel when it comes to your skills and talents. Take this confidence with you into the moments where you're questioning yourself or listening to your inner critical voice. Focus on the feelings of confidence, as this will help boost your self-esteem and allow you to see everything that you can learn.

You should spend more time at the gym or start an at-home exercise routine. There are several psychological studies that focus on how staying active improves your self-esteem because it's correlated to your mental health.

When you take time to make your body feel good, your mind starts to feed off of this emotion.

Lastly, one of the most important steps you can take is also seen as one of the hardest—forgiveness. It's important to not only forgive other people, no matter what they did, but also forgive yourself. For example, if you've left an abusive relationship, you'll find yourself asking, "Why did I stay?" The answer to this is complicated but it often makes you feel like you failed yourself. Now you think about the long road of recovery you have, and you can't help but get angry at yourself and the person who abused you. It takes time to reach a state of forgiveness in these difficult times, but it's important to work toward it because what happened isn't your fault. It's a learning experience that you can take with you to keep yourself from that situation again and use it to help others who find themselves in a similar story.

Once you start focusing on building your self-esteem, you'll notice how your life begins to improve. Your self-confidence will start to flourish, and you'll find yourself reaching your goals and aiming higher.

"Don't confuse a part with the whole. Nobody is completely good. Or completely bad. Reaffirm the good things about yourself and go over the things that make you feel bad. And always remember that you can change the bad things." - Bernardo Stamateas (Exploring Your Mind, 2016).

Reasons to Listen to Your Intuition

You've probably heard the phrase, "trust your intuition" many times. However, no one really explains why. You know that it means you need to listen to the feeling you have in your gut that tells you to do or not do something. For example, you might have a feeling of dread before you're about to spontaneously take a new route to work. But why do you have this feeling?

One of the main reasons you should listen is because your gut determines what is safe for you through your past experiences. In a sense, it has its own memory card and works with your brain to remember what happened the last time you made a similar decision. Did it end well, or did you find yourself making a mistake? If it didn't end well, your gut will more than likely tell you not to do it again.

Another reason is because your nerve cells and your intuition work together. This happens because the subconscious mind is sending signals to the nerve cells in your abdomen, which makes you feel like there are butterflies in your stomach. Listening to the feeling allows you to make a decision with your whole body instead of just your brain.

Some people believe that intuition is more powerful than listening to other people and their advice because it's encoded with facts and emotions. Your gut doesn't just connect to your mind but also your spirit and the rest of your body. It will give you a sense of calm when everything is fine, excitement during a new chapter in your life, or worry if something is wrong.

Another reason intuition prevails is because it allows you to come up with original solutions to problems. Your gut can combine your past experiences, emotions, and what you've learned to help you overcome a challenge. It gives you that inner voice in your head that is typically right when it comes to deciding what you should and shouldn't do. Even when you don't want to hear what it says, it's your inner wisdom and is there to help guide you through life so you can learn from your past, make better decisions in your future, and reach your ultimate potential.

The Power of Positive Thinking: Mindful Habits for Creating a Positive Life

Positive thinking is powerful. It helps you create healthy habits, set the right goals, and supports you in achieving them. You establish a solid emotional and psychological foundation that changes the way you view yourself and how you interact with other people. It boosts your self-confidence and self-esteem.

The challenge is you need to transform your thinking. It's not as easy as going to a book of affirmations and reading a quote. You need to believe what you're reading and make the appropriate changes in your life. It's easier said than done, which makes you wonder if something is wrong or if you're immune to positive thinking.

The truth is, you have a choice. You need to make the effort and embrace the benefits of an optimistic mindset. There are many ways to incorporate this power into your everyday life. For example, you can choose to tell yourself "for every negative thought I have, I will give myself two positive ones." As long as you follow through every day, you'll establish this habit. You can also surround yourself with people who want to see you succeed and bring you happiness. Making a conscious decision to only watch uplifting movies and listen to joyous music is another way.

The struggle is you'll find yourself moving back to your old way of thinking without realising it. For instance, you're driving to work and hear a news story on the radio that makes you angry. You start to think about how awful the people are and how hateful the world has become. When you get to work, your mood is sour, and you don't want to talk to anyone. You wish for the day to be over as soon as possible so you can go home and hide from the cruel world. An hour later your emotions begin to calm down and you realise how quick you were to judge others and how swiftly you allowed the negativity to consume part of your morning. At this moment, you need to be gentle with yourself and take your mind back to positive thoughts. You might start by finding the heroes in the news story or think of a happy memory.

Words are powerful. They can make a path for your positive thinking or create a mountain blocking the way. The language you use verbally and nonverbally affects your view of yourself, the people around you, and your surroundings. You can start to change your mindset by focusing on the words you use. To practise, you can decide to set aside two hours a day where you focus on only saying and thinking positive words. You want to use phrases that will strip the negativity from your soul and enhance your positive mindset.

Make a stop at your local library after work and look for books that can help you transform your thoughts. For example, you might find a book of motivational essays, affirmations, or one to help you learn how to choose your thoughts through strategies.

Tune into your consciousness so you can become more mindful of your thought pattern. You can build on this mindset by finding strategies to help you focus and think about your behaviour. When you're sitting in a meeting, don't allow yourself to daydream. Instead, pay close attention to what your coworkers say, take notes, and engage in conversation. When you're driving your normal route, take note of the landscapes you pass. You can also count cars of a certain colour.

The more you practise positive thinking, the more powerful you'll feel. You'll start to learn more about yourself by pushing through your fears and overcoming your challenges. You'll know that your opportunities are endless.

Self-Care Tips That Are Tough but Life-Changing

When you think about self-care, you imagine binge watching your favourite Netflix show or eating comfort food, which is great in the short-term, but you also need to consider long-term care. You must look at what makes you feel better internally. It's not always easy. In fact, you might feel that it's uncomfortable and want to ignore it even though it makes you feel relaxed. The key is to incorporate these tips into your life gradually. Once you start, you'll find that they become more comfortable and eventually transform your life.

Going to therapy. There are many reasons why you might feel uncomfortable going to therapy. After all, it requires you to talk to a stranger about your personal details. It leaves you feeling vulnerable and stressed, but I promise that you'll feel better over time. Whether you need someone to help work out daily problems or childhood trauma, there's a type of therapy suited for it. Therapists can help you in ways that your friends and family can't because they're trained to help people through difficult times and emotions.

Ending toxic relationships. Anyone can bring toxicity into your life, from a parent to a colleague. The trouble is, it's easier to step away from a negative coworker than it is to ask your mum, dad, brother, sister, or friend for space. It's harder to tell them how they're draining your energy or causing you problems. You feel like you're always in competition with them and walking on eggshells. One of the biggest steps is to distance yourself from them. Start with talking to them but if they don't respond well or refuse to change, end the relationship. Walking away sounds easier than it is, but it's essential to do this because you need to prioritise yourself.

Enjoying being alone. Do you enjoy being alone or do you feel like you're lonely? Do you feel guilty when you request silence from your children or alone time? You might find that you avoid solitude because you don't like the feeling you get from it. You start to think that you're ignoring people, wonder what will happen if there is an emergency, or that you're being selfish. It's important to get comfortable with your "me time" because it allows you to get to know yourself better.

Do what you enjoy. Of course, you'll always have responsibilities that aren't your favourite. Even if you love your job there will be one or two tasks you'd rather ignore and put off for as long as possible. But if your work makes you feel miserable, it's time to look at another route. Ask yourself what you want to do in your life—what is your main purpose? What is your dream job? What will make you want to jump out of bed every morning? Once you have an idea, start making your plans and set goals to get there. You can accomplish anything you set your mind to so get started on what you enjoy.

Stop apologising for everything. How many times a day do you say "I'm sorry" or feel like something is your fault? Compassion is a great trait, but you shouldn't apologise when you've done nothing wrong. When you feel the urge, stop and ask yourself if it's necessary. You will probably notice that most of the time you're empathising with someone and want them to know that you understand their emotions. Instead of aiming for the two common words, tell them something that's more comforting. Even if it's, "I understand" or "I don't understand, but I hear you and I'm here for you."

Learn to say no. Saying no to someone, especially your boss, friend, or family member who needs your help is a challenge. You want to do everything you can to please them but often this pushes your self-care to the side. In return, you start to feel overwhelmed and irritated. Learn what your limits are and if you feel like the project is too much, say "no." Furthermore, remember that the word "no" is a sentence in itself. You don't need to explain why you can't do something; you just need to politely decline.

To the Highly Sensitive and the Empath: You're Abilities Are a Blessing

Highly sensitive people and empaths are sometimes viewed as "too emotional." You're put in this category where some people believe that you need to "toughen up" and learn to "deal with life." Every day is not a picnic, and you know this. In fact, you understand this better than many other people.

You might see that your ability to feel everything so deeply is more of a curse, but it's a blessing that can help change the world. You carry a diamond in your heart and soul that other people don't have. It's important that you take care of your gift so you can shower the world around you with compassion and understanding.

You feel emotions at a deeper level, and you have this natural ability to understand them. They might come to you in the pit of your stomach or your chest, making it hard to breathe. You might feel the urge to cry when you walk into a room. You meet someone on the street and get this twinge of emotion that tells you they're feeling lost and lonely.

You turn away from social media because you can't understand or tolerate all of the negativity. You can't watch violence, see someone suffer, dying, or crying.

Everything you hear, smell, taste, and feel is more intense.

Sometimes this becomes too much and you want to run away from it all. Other times you feel that you're alone and don't know who to communicate with about it. You have this urge to express your emotions, to understand them, to learn to let go but you feel that you'll only become a burden to someone trying to help you.

You might feel that all hope is lost. You choose to hide alone in your room because loneliness is easier to manage than the world around you.

When you're an empath or highly sensitive, you have a different set of challenges, but you also have a superpower. It's time to take control of your strength, learn to release your built-up emotions, and share your gift.

Embrace your blessing and be proud of your superpower. Shine your light brightly wherever you go.

Learn How to Fall Forward

Do you find yourself constantly replaying your mistakes in your head? You might do this when you're trying to fall asleep or about to try to complete the task again. Mistakes are a part of life. They're something that everyone does, but this doesn't make it easier. You might feel embarrassed or belittle yourself. You tell yourself that you couldn't do it right the first time so why try again? Why—because you want to fall forward.

Instead of letting your mistakes hold you back, use them as stepping stones to your goals. Instead of seeing them as something you did wrong, see them as a learning experience so you can continue to grow.

Sometimes telling yourself to fall forward is easier said than done, but it's never impossible. To help yourself move past your mistake, set up a system to follow. When you're facing failure, ask yourself these questions.

1. What went wrong? Think about the situation and notice everything that you feel went wrong. If you're working alongside teammates, ask them for their input as well. You want to be honest with yourself, even when it's not easy.
2. What went right? It's not that you failed on every step in the project; rather, the outcome was simply different from what you planned. Just as you did in the first step, do here. But this time,

focus on everything that went well. Don't forget to praise yourself for the small victories because you deserve it.

3. Why did certain steps go wrong? Now that you have an understanding of what went right and wrong, ask yourself why it happened this way. This can be a hard question to answer because you might not fully comprehend the process. Take a few steps back, if needed, and go through the whole project again. Walk through it slowly and talk it out to yourself or your team. Did it have to do with the process itself? Did you make wrong assumptions? Did you start to speed through a certain step and miss something important? Sometimes you need to think outside the box or request assistance when it comes to this step.

4. Are there repeating mistakes? Make sure that you're not repeating any mistakes. Sometimes, you don't even realise what truly happened because as you were working, your mind switched to autopilot. Look through the process mindfully and leave your attitude about mistakes at the door. You need to look at it as a lesson that can help you develop your skills. If you constantly focus on the word "mistake" and

what you did wrong, you won't notice valuable information that will help you fall forward.
5. Can you salvage your project, or do you need to start from scratch? Look at the outcome and observe what is available to reuse and what you need to completely do over. For instance, can you use the same data or equipment? This will help you get started on your project again.

As you're going through these steps you need to pay attention to your emotions. It's often the way we feel that keeps our mind on the cycle of "I made a mistake. I can't believe I did this." When you feel that you're becoming overwhelmed with negative emotions, take a break or work on a different project. You might need to focus on calming or breathing exercises to help you regain your focus. Don't make rash decisions or judgements at any point in this process because it will only escalate your negativity toward mistakes.

Realise Your Full Potential by Conquering Your Fears

Fear is one of the most powerful emotions in you. It's one that tends to pop up continuously throughout the day. In fact, sometimes you're not even aware that it's happening. For example, you're in a shop looking for your next project and come across the paint section. You've always imagined yourself painting a masterpiece that you can hang on the wall. You enjoy drawing and believe you're good at it, but you've never tried your talents with painting. As you pick up some canvas and look over it you become aware of the price. You then start thinking about how much money you would waste on supplies if the painting doesn't turn out. You think to yourself how embarrassing it would be to tell your family and friends you're painting a portrait and then realise it's of poor quality. You think about everything that can go wrong, so you set the canvas back down and head to a different aisle.

Why did you start thinking this way? Is it because you have very little experience with painting? This is probably what you tell yourself but if you are honest, it's because you started to feel fear. You began to fear embarrassment and failure.

You let the way you felt stop you from trying. You're an artist, you love to draw, and you can easily switch from pens to paint. You could learn the differences in your movements and how it works to succeed in your dreams, but fear held you back so now you won't realise your full potential. Fortunately, there are several tips to help you overcome this challenge so you can learn more about your skills and talents.

Ask yourself why you're afraid. Is there something from your past that makes you scared to try something new now? Think about everything that holds you back from trying something new or different. For example, do you worry about going back to school because of the changes your family will need to adjust to? Are you afraid of leaving a stable job to start your own business? This is a step where you learn more about yourself and start to realise that you're creating your own fears.

Think positive. One of the biggest reasons people put fear into their mind is because they lack self-confidence. They don't think positively about the situation. Use affirmations or imagine yourself succeeding to help you move beyond your fears and worries. This step is a process in itself so it might take you some time. Unfortunately, choosing your thoughts doesn't happen overnight. It takes effort to learn how to acknowledge your fears, push them aside, and then think in a positive direction.

Switch your language. How many times a day do you say to yourself, "I can't" or something similarly defeatist? They might just seem like words to you, but they're powerful. When you tell yourself that you "can't" do something, you will start to believe it. Instead of telling yourself that it won't work, you need to say it will work. You need to tell yourself that you *can* do it.

Start smaller. Instead of purchasing a large canvas to pain, start by painting on cardboard or paper. Begin on a smaller scale and work your way up toward your dreams. This allows you to start building your confidence, so you realise your full potential.

Your Pain Can Help You Grow

Pain is unavoidable. No matter how much you want to ignore the difficult moments of your life, it's not possible. You'll hurt yourself and other people will hurt you. You'll feel physical, emotional, and psychological pain more than you want to admit.

You believe pain is bad because you see it as a negative puzzle piece in your life. But, it's possible that pain can become a catalyst for your growth. I wrote a lot about this in my article "[Use Your Pain As A Catalyst for Growth]" on *Thought Catalog*. I ask that you read this article as well as this book, because you'll receive the most valuable information to help you thrive with your pain.

When you feel pain, whether it's emotional, physical, or mental you want to see it as a crack that lets in light. Think of what it's like to see the sunlight through the bottom of the door or a crack in the curtains. The same type of light seeps into your soul when you're hurt.

To let more light in you need to learn to channel your pain, which you can do through these three steps.

1. **Get to know your feelings.** Find a way that will let you explore your emotions. You might do this through therapy, journaling, or talking to a friend. Do more than simply tell yourself or someone else how you feel—get in touch with

them. Understand why they came to you during this time. What caused you to feel this way and why? Did your loved one criticise you? Did you take what they said personally or negatively, even though they were trying to help you do well on your project? The trick is to dig as deeply as you can. Do you feel this way because of a situation in your childhood or past relationship? Is it because you struggle with low self-esteem or confidence?

2. **What lesson can you take from your pain?** After you understand your emotions and where they come from, it's time to look at what you can learn from them. Is it time that you start improving your self-confidence by learning to move on from a painful past, so it doesn't continue to hold you back? This is another step that can become difficult because it's not easy to dig into the depths of your soul. It's hard to admit that you harmed yourself or that someone you loved dearly caused you pain. You might realise that what you need to do is take a step back and re-evaluate your priorities so you can overcome your illness or move forward from your current problem. It might take you a while to notice the lesson. If you believe that there is

something you can learn from every difficult situation, you'll find one in the process.
3. **Make the conscious decision to change.** By now you have an idea of how you can use your pain to bring you further into your future. When you think about the lessons you're learning, decide how you can make changes in your life. If you need assistance to help you focus on your adjustments or come up with a plan, reach out to a therapist. If you feel that you need to modify your priorities or find a different career path so you can reach your happiness, come up with a list of steps to help you succeed in this mission.

By working from the stem, you can turn your pain into power.

25 Reminders You Are Enough

You might think you need to lose weight and fit into a size 6, you might think you need a shinier car, the latest smartphone and the fanciest house decor. You might think you will not be deemed okay if you don't buy more, show more, are more.

But I am here to tell you that you, my dear, are more than enough. Here are 25 reminders to look at when you feel you have struggled for too long and have dealt with too much.

1. Nobody Can Be Everything

You might think you have to be everything. That you have to wear the perfect size and the perfect clothes, live in the picture-perfect house and build a movie-worthy, perfect life.

The absolute truth is that you don't have to do any of this. Nobody can be everything—so pick your battles, fight them with fierceness, and win at whatever you set your mind to. One goal at a time.

2. Nobody Can Be Flawless

All those pretty ladies on TV and on Insta? All those buffed up guys in gym magazines?

They do exist, and they sure work hard for their looks. But even so, everything you see through the looking glass of the TV, internet, and media are just bits and pieces of what those people's lives truly are.

They might look shiny, successful, and super-happy in their flawless bodies, houses, and cars. Yet, you will never actually know just how happy they are. The astounding number of celebrities suffering from depression proves it: you can be flawless and have everything, but happiness is not a matter of quantity or beauty standards.

3. Social Media Is, Well, a Lie

If you scroll down on your Facebook feed, it might appear like everyone else is doing better than you. On social media, all of your former high school classmates are CEOs, medical doctors, movie stars and supermodels. They also somehow manage to be perfect parents, own the most adorable little pups and kittens, and find the time to cook intricate dishes every other day.

Social media is a lie because it allows you to see just what those people want you to see. Behind closed doors, most people have their own problems. It's just that they don't vent them out into your social media feed.

4. Mistakes Are Okay

Mistakes are so natural it would be foolish to believe someone would be godlike enough not to make them.

There is a very good reason you should believe mistakes are Okay. Beyond the fact that you really need to be more forgiving with yourself and show yourself more compassion, mistakes are okay because that's how we learn. We are programmed to learn in a handful of ways, one of which is exactly this: life bloopers.

5. Taking the Wrong Path Is Okay Too

It's okay to not know exactly where you want to be five years from now (like everyone is asked at every single job interview under the Sun).

It's also more than okay to switch your path and do whatever you please. Yes, you might have spent years doing a specific "something," but it's never too late to change your mind and pursue a different road in your personal or professional life. NOBODY should ever have to spend the rest of their lives feeling miserable just because they have invested time, effort, emotion, and/or financial resources into something that did not work out.

6. Authenticity Is Worth More Than a Billion Dollars

Be authentic. Be yourself not because you have "no other choice," but because it is the most amazing person to be.

Authenticity can be defined in many ways, but the most wonderful thing about it is that you get to define your own sense of authenticity. So allow yourself to be.

7. Happiness Has Nothing to Do With Everything Outside

Nobody can define your happiness better, more accurately, and more astoundingly beautiful than you.

Happiness is not something you buy at the mall, nor is it a diploma or an extra zero on your paycheck. It is a state of mind. When you finally accept that happiness comes from within, you have won.

8. People Are People

Don't let anyone put you down, directly or indirectly. People are people—meaning they too are flawed, and they too might hurt someone. That's okay. Forgive and forget, but don't allow yourself to be swept down into the dark pit of holding grudges against anyone.

Even more, don't allow yourself to stay when you should be leaving. Nobody is ever allowed to intoxicate you with their own negativity—so if you feel a place or a person is not good for you, then accept that you have the right to leave. No questions asked.

9. You Are Strong

You might be crying, and you might feel lost. You might even feel on the brink of a moral and emotional collapse.

These are not moments of weakness, though, but more like a forest you have to go through to shine brighter on the other side.

Every bump in the road is an occasion for you to turn into a real-life Phoenix: to rise from your ashes and astound everyone with the entirety of your being.

10. You Are Stunning

Beauty is in the eye of the beholder. It truly is. So the next time you look in the mirror and start picking at your flames, remember that you are stunning. Weight, nose sizes, eye colour, hair length—they have nothing to do with beauty. They are social standards. And if we have to be honest, they change quite a lot.

Just look at how the "perfect woman" was defined 200 years ago and look at where we are now.

You are gorgeous just the way you are. Take care of your health, eat nutritious meals, move, and pamper yourself—but know that no silly social standards can ever tell you that you are not beautiful enough.

11. You Have the Power to Fight

You really do. Just like we are wired to learn by making mistakes, we are also wired to fight. That's how our species survived, in the end. We learned how to fight using our best weapons and we rose to the top of the food chain.

Being a fighter is in your DNA.

12. More Things Will Never Make You Happy

Buying "stuff" will never make you truly happy. It might give you a moment of joy and excitement, but as mentioned before, happiness is a state of mind.

Happiness stems from how you take care of yourself and how you learn to detach yourself from the pain and suffering, which are exterior to you. Happiness begins when you accept that there are things you cannot change. And that's okay.

13. Failure Is Just a Stepping Stone, Anyway

If you look at every single successful person in the history of the world, you will very easily see a very clear pattern: they all failed, at some point.

This circles us back to the fact that mistakes are more than okay. Failure is also okay, precisely because it is a stepping stone and a purifying fire on the way to success.

14. Heartbreak Happens

You cannot control how someone else feels about you, no matter how much you try. As such, heartbreak is bound to happen, sooner or later in life, in ways that are more or less irreparable.

Accept that you will have your heart broken, but don't let that prevent you from enjoying the ride. Love is amazing even when it hurts, so embrace it as it is, and take your positive thoughts with you when you close the door behind you.

15. Abuse Happens

Abuse has nothing to do with how accomplished you are in your career or how much money you have in your bank account.

It happens. And you have to move away from it when it does, to allow yourself to heal and rebuild.

16. You Don't Have to Settle

This is especially true for women, but men, too, might feel pressured into settling.

That is the last thing you want to do, though. Settling just for the sake of settling will only bring misery and pain on both ends of the spectrum. Don't settle. Be curious, search, experience everything and settle on something or someone when you truly feel that it is right.

17. You Cannot Predict the Future

No matter how much you plan, you cannot predict the future. As such, it is important for you to accept that some things will happen and you might not be fully prepared for them.

That's okay. It is, as I was saying earlier, out of your control.

18. You Can Change Everything

You have the power to change whatever you set your mind to, precisely because fighting is in your DNA.

Whatever makes you unhappy now can be turned around and tossed away to be replaced with something that brings you genuine peace and everlasting joy.

19. Fashion Comes and Fashion Goes

You really don't have to dress a certain way to be beautiful, successful, or worthy.

You do you. Fashion comes and fashion goes, and there's really not much you can do about it if you don't like it.

20. You Deserve Love. The Truest Kind

Everyone deserves love, and you are no exception. We are created by love and we deserve to be loved in a pure, true, and absolute way.

You deserve love that makes you laugh, and that respects you; love that makes you giggle when you think of it; love that makes you feel pleasure and joy; love that embraces every inch of your body, mind, and soul.

21. You Are Worthy of Happiness

Just like you are worthy of love, you are also worthy of happiness (which you may or may not define through the perspective of love).

No matter who you are and where you come from, you absolutely deserve to be happy. Don't let anyone make you think anything else.

22. Success Is Really a Matter of Choice

No, we are not "wired" to be unsuccessful or mediocre. We are wired to win, precisely because we are fighters and because we deserve everything good.

You make the choice. Are you going to be successful?

23. Being Vulnerable Is Okay

Being a fighter has nothing to do with hiding behind a wall of emotionless faces and actions.

Being vulnerable is more than okay, it is what makes us beautifully human and wonderfully flawed.

Allow yourself to be vulnerable every once in a while. It will make you feel alive.

24. You Are Gifted With Beauty Everywhere You Look

If you know how to look, you can find beauty everywhere you turn your head. A flower, the smile of someone you love, the taste of a cupcake, the memories of your childhood—they are all beautiful and you have the power to look at them through your own perspective to make them yours.

25. You Are the Only One Who Is… YOU

The most important reason you are enough?

Well, you are enough because you are the only one who is YOU. As such, you get to define your worth, your success, your pains, and your struggles. You get to define your beauty standards and your timing. You get to define who you settle for and whether or not you do it.

You are the only one who is YOU. And you have something truly unique to offer to this world. You deserve to love yourself first and foremost!

"We all have waves that cross the surface of our lives caused by others or ourselves intentionally or unintentionally. If we didn't have these ripples our lives would be flat and boring. Embrace it all."
- Amy Reis Williams

Chapter 2:

Ripples

When you see the word "ripples," think of throwing a rock in calm water and take note of what happens. Ripples form in the water from the location the rock hit and spread out. They continue to run, going further away from the centre, which is where the rock first landed on the water. Even when you can no longer see the rock, the ripples still continue to form.

It's important to understand the impact one action has because it will create a ripple effect throughout your life and even into the lives of other people. For example, you drive by a car lot and see they have a vehicle you've wanted for years. You know the price tag is higher than you can afford but it's calling your name. After talking to the car salesperson, you learn that there is a lot of interest, so you decide to give them a down payment and connect with your bank on a loan. Once you sign the papers, you take a deep breath and realise that you still need to explain your actions to your partner. You now have to sit down and create a new monthly budget. The actions you made have a positive and negative ripple effect for you and your family.

Yes, ripples can be both negative and positive. For example, you're the first generation in your family to graduate from a university is a ripple that will positively affect other people in your family. It increases the likelihood that your children, any younger siblings, or cousins, will graduate, and you might even inspire the someone from the older generation to go to a university.

It's important to realise that sometimes ripples can continue to form years later, if not decades. If you grew up with an abusive parent and you carry certain effects with you into your children's lives, it's a ripple. Your childhood helps establish the core person you become. It doesn't mean that you stop growing and developing as a person, it means that you'll carry certain pieces of your childhood with you into your adult life. This will start to affect other people, such as your friends, partner, and children. It can also affect the way you think about yourself, how you handle problems, and your work ethic.

Don't feel that once ripples start to flow that you can't stop them. The essays below are full of ways to help you learn and grow from the little waves in your life.

The Ripples of Psychological Trauma and Its Effects

Have you ever heard the phrase "life happens?" It's usually stated after your plans fall apart. You carefully go through every step, and when it seems that everything is coming together, it breaks into a million little pieces and you're left to pick them up. Most people think trauma occurs after a bad event that causes you to emotionally or mentally suffer for a period of time, but this isn't necessarily true. Trauma happens when your brain has felt so much stress that it causes damage. This can happen when you lose a loved one, job, or your home. It can even happen through social events, such as terrorist attacks.

You feel that the event is centred on you. When you have a family, you try hard not to make them aware of your stress. You try to ensure that your children's schedule continues like normal. You spend your time doing everything you can to make the situation and any adjustments easier for everyone else. Unfortunately, your immediate family and even other loved ones and friends can feel the ripples. They feel your emotions and they want to help you but don't know how. This affects them deeply and can cause waves to go further into their personal lives.

It's not just the people in your life who are affected. Your goals, thought patterns, routine, and anything you do can also feel the ripples. For example, if you lose your job because you made a mistake in a project, your self-confidence declines and this makes you think negatively. Soon, you find that all you do is focus on what goes wrong in your life and you forget to look at the positives. From here your future work positions can feel the effects. You'll start to treat people differently, even strangers or retail employees. You can even find yourself struggling to hold on to your marriage.

One of the biggest problems with ripples is they have no idea when to stop, so you have to do what you can to end them. You can do this by following these steps:

1. Take time out of your day to breathe. You can do this through meditation or exercises where you focus on taking slow deep breaths. Sometimes the best moments to follow this strategy is when you're starting to feel stressed or overwhelmed.
2. Let go of self-blame by learning about how your body functions under stress. Find a way to normalise yourself with the stress so you can monitor your emotions and stay in control of your actions.
3. Realise that this is just a piece to your life's puzzle. Even though it looks like it's the end of the world, you will move on to better and

brighter days. You will overcome this challenge. You are okay.
4. Look for ways to diffuse the psychological trauma. Talk to other people who have had similar experiences or with a therapist. Write about your situation and look for ways you can turn it into a positive.

When You Fail, Fall Forward

How do you handle failure? Have you ever wondered why some people handle it better than others? For example, some people will stop doing everything they were working on when faced with failure. They will need time to adjust to the news and might show sadness, anger, or frustration. Other people will accept what happened and continue working on their tasks and goals. On the other side, it's like they don't even care, but they do. They have just learned that instead of letting defeat hold them back they need to fall forward.

Talking about how you need to fall forward and actually doing it are two separate steps. It's a lot easier to let the words roll off your tongue than it is to incorporate the actions into your life. But by following some of the tips below you'll find that you adjust to failure better over time.

Accept reality. The hardest part is usually the first step to falling forward. You need to admit to yourself that you failed. Accepting reality makes it easier for you to start moving forward, but it takes time. You might continue to try to fix the problem or go over all of the "what ifs." You might even wonder what you did wrong because you don't truly understand. When you get to the point where you accept your reality, you'll feel like a 1,000-pound weight was lifted off your shoulders and you'll be free to carry on to your next step.

Don't have regrets. There's an old saying that goes, "Life is too short to have regrets." It's true! You might not realise how short and precious life is right now, but you will soon, and then you'll comprehend that there is no room for regrets. This doesn't mean that you won't have a few seconds of a "I wish I would've done this instead" moment; it means that you'll accept that thought and then move on. You know there is nothing you can do to change it now so why worry about it when you can focus on brighter moments ahead.

Don't treat yourself like a victim. It's easy to find yourself catching the "woe-is-me" attitude when something doesn't work in your favour. You start to treat yourself like a victim and feed into your negativity. Take notice of this behaviour and change your mindset toward fixing the strategy. Ask yourself a series of questions like "What didn't work?" "What mistakes did I make?" and "What can I do next time to improve my process?" If you need to, talk to your colleagues or others who can help you find a better plan.

Treat failure as a lesson you needed to learn. From the moment you came into this world, there are lessons that you had to learn. You didn't have a choice, especially if you wanted to reach your goals. One way to accomplish this task is to treat every day like it's a school day and you have a lesson to learn. Challenge yourself to learn something new every day. Then, take notice of everything else that is new to you by making a mental note or writing them down. At the end of the day, reflect on all the knowledge you gained and focus on how it can improve your game plan.

How You Can Master Your Reactions to Stress

You open your eyes, look at the clock, and notice the time. You leap out of bed and grab your phone. You forgot to set the alarm and now you'll be late for work. You rush to get the children up for school and give them a quick breakfast. You're trying to balance getting everyone ready and find yourself constantly checking the time, which only increases your stress. Then, one of your children says they can't find their homework. As you're running to their room to help them look, you start feeling like you can't breathe. You place your hand on your chest and start to take a few deep breaths. You don't want to worry your family, so you know you need to keep your anxiety under control. Fortunately, the homework is found, and everyone is packed into the car to go to school and work. You make it to work right on time and realise that everything is fine. In fact, you learn that your boss is also running late. But, you still can't shake off your stress, which you feel the rest of the day.

Why does stress tend to cling on for hours, days, weeks, and sometimes months or longer? Even when the situation ends, why do you still feel stressed and anxious? It has to do with all of the psychological and biological effects.

Biologically, you might have a headache as your heart feels like it'll pop out of your chest. Your breathing can become heavy, you might grind your teeth and clench your jaw. Other effects include difficulty swallowing, feeling a lump in your throat, sweaty palms, dizziness, high blood pressure, fatigue, upset stomach and feeling like your muscles are twitching.

Psychologically you become irritable. You focus on the worst-case scenario and your thought pattern is negative. You feel overwhelmed, overworked, have a sense of helplessness, lack a sense of humour and can be jumpy. You have trouble focusing as your mind isn't clear. You feel that you can't think straight, and your brain is cluttered. Your relationships with friends, family and coworkers starts to decline as you fail to set aside time for the hobbies you enjoy. You begin to pull yourself away from society and start to feel lonely.

It's normal to feel stressed during certain times in your life, such as adjusting to changes or financial setbacks. The negative effects become a problem when you're chronically stressed and struggle to find peace. Unfortunately, it's easy to live with stress every day of your life because of a busy schedule. Therefore, you want to find ways to master your stress so you can live your life to the fullest.

- Find time for nature by going for a walk or sitting down in a quiet location. Enjoy the silence you hear and the warmth of the sun. You might have a favourite spot or simply follow your gut to know where to go.
- Go out for lunch by yourself or with a friend, but don't rush. Take your time ordering, eating, and enjoy the conversation.
- Practise breathing exercises by taking slow and deep breaths. You can close your eyes and imagine a sensation of peace entering your nose

as you inhale and then release tension out of your mouth every time you exhale.
- If you feel a connection to the universe, take time to go outside at night and look at the stars or learn about numerology.
- Spend time doing something calming that you enjoy like reading, journaling or watching a movie.
- Express your emotions through painting, drawing or writing.
- Focus on the moment by noticing your senses and what you're doing. If you're at work think about how you sit in your desk chair and how that makes your back, hips, and rest of your body feel.

Once you find primary ways to help you destress in the moment, you'll notice more peace in your environment. One of the biggest blessings of this is that the feeling will follow you around wherever you go, allowing you to help other people find their comfort and peace.

25 Affirmations to Begin Your Day With Positive Ripples

Remember, everything you do creates ripples. The thoughts you have in the morning can affect your mood for the rest of the day. If you wake up and dread something you have to do, you'll feel anxious. If you take time to focus on positivity, such as reading different affirmations, you'll feel more thankful.

To understand how it works, you need to know the benefits. Some of them you'll notice right away while others you'll feel after a few days. Through affirmations you will increase your problem-solving skills, positive emotions, relationships, ability to reach personal success, and you'll become more aware of your thought patterns. You'll also reduce anxiety and stress, establish inner clarity, and build your confidence.

It's important to realise that you need to do more than simply read the quote in front of you. You need to believe what you're reading and use the power of repetition. Once you start, take time to do this every day. You can even say the affirmation more than once. You might even write it down and keep it in your pocket so you can look at it throughout the day. Choose one that resonates with your mood or a situation you're going through. It also helps to say it out loud, even if you feel a little silly doing so as this will pass over time.

Here are a few to help you begin your morning habit:

1. I choose happiness because I am in charge of how I feel.
2. I accept myself just as I am.
3. Today, I will focus on the joy in my heart.
4. I will choose to treat others with compassion today.
5. I will stop comparing myself to other people.
6. Today, I will focus on patience.
7. I am grateful for everything in my life.
8. I am thankful for the lessons I am learning.
9. I will treat every day as a blessing because that's exactly what it is.
10. Today, I choose to let go of all the negativity in my life and focus on positivity.
11. I am the narrator of my life.
12. I trust that I will make the right decisions because my intuition always guides me correctly.
13. Today, I choose to feel motivated.
14. I will surround myself with people who support me and bring happiness into my life.
15. I will celebrate each goal I reach with pride.
16. I have the willpower and courage to change my mindset to focus on the positive.
17. When I am me, I am free and happy.

18. I will believe in myself because this will teach other people to believe in me.
19. I am reaching my goals and living my life to my full potential.
20. I have all the tools I need to make today a wonderful day.
21. Today I will choose self-love.
22. Every day I discover something new to help improve my life.
23. Today I choose to be open-minded as it will help me reach my desired success.
24. My confidence is rising because I acknowledge my self-worth.
25. I am feeling confident and loved.

Signs You Might Be in an Emotionally Abusive Relationship

One of the biggest psychological and emotional ripples comes from abusive relationships. It doesn't matter if you're in a physically or emotionally abusive relationship; from the moment it begins, the ripples will form, and they will extend outside of your body and mind without you realising it. For example, you'll start to treat your friends and family differently, possibly even stop communication. You'll bring your emotional baggage to work and find that you're less productive. You might face the struggles of meeting deadlines or trying to work with others while you're internally bruised and battered. It's a feeling that you wish you didn't have to face and one that you wouldn't wish on your worst enemy.

But there are many people who don't even realise that they're in an abusive relationship, especially on the emotional level. The main reason for this is because emotional abuse is hard to recognise. It's more confusing to you because you can believe the behaviours from your abuser are normal. You might also be used to harsh criticism or bullying because you faced it throughout your childhood. Another reason is because your abuser was kind and gentle at the beginning of the relationship. Gradually, they started to change their behaviour, but you don't catch on because you transform along with their words and actions.

Emotional abuse is meant to give the abuser power over the victim. It's a way they can assert their control over you without you realising what is happening. There are many symptoms of abuse, such as gaslighting, shaming, insulting, threatening, lying, ignoring, and intimidating. The scars aren't visible to the human eye, but you feel the effects through lower self-esteem, Post Traumatic Stress Disorder (PTSD), anxiety, substance abuse, and depression.

To help you better understand emotional abuse, here are some of the most common signs:

Gaslighting is when you're manipulated by someone psychologically in a way that causes you to question your sanity. One of the most common examples is when you hear your abuser say something and when you bring it up to them again, they tell you that they never said that or that you were the one who said it. This happens so many times that you start to question your reality. You start to wonder if you're truly seeing what you remember or if you're making it up. They deny or distort reality so they can twist your perception to support their reality.

You apologise even when you did nothing wrong. You might know that your partner made the mistake, but they will blame you and expect an apology. In the beginning, you start questioning and evening arguing with them but soon learn that it's easier to just apologise. Soon, you start finding yourself saying "I'm sorry" to behaviours you didn't even do because you start to believe that you're selfish or inconsiderate. You start to believe that everything is your fault.

You walk on eggshells. You don't want to disturb your partner when you get up in the middle of the night because it makes them angry. You want to ensure that you have a meal ready when they come home from work, that the home is clean, and do whatever you can to ensure they're happy—no matter how it makes you feel. You push your feelings aside because you can handle them, but you can't handle your partner's outbursts when they're angry or frustrated. When you reach this symptom, you're internalising the emotional abuse so your partner doesn't need to act. This isn't a sign that will start right away, it usually begins after several outbursts or months of abusive behaviour.

Your partner disguises his hurtful comments as jokes. If your significant other ever says something that emotionally hurts you and tells you that they were "just joking" or asks, "Can't you take a joke?" they're giving you a sign of emotional abuse. Someone who doesn't want to hurt you in any way won't defend their words as a joke. Instead, they will apologise and watch what they say more closely so they don't make you feel bad.

You need to check-in often. If your partner demands that you check-in with them regularly, wants to know everything you're doing, or everyone you're with you could be in an abusive relationship. Even if you believe they're concerned or that it's part of being in a relationship, it's their way to gain more control over you.

There are many other signs such as your abuser doesn't compliment you, they talk down to you, and withhold affection. The moment you start to wonder if you're in an emotionally abusive relationship, it's time to look at it through another lens. Ask yourself what you would tell your friends or family if they were in a similar situation. If you notice your behaviour changing and you're focusing on more negative thoughts, it's time to ask yourself why.

Once you realise you're struggling with emotional abuse, it's time to figure out an action plan. If you can't talk to your partner and they won't seek counselling, focus on yourself and do what you need to do for your mental health. Realise that you don't deserve this relationship and help is there for you. You're not alone. There are many people who want to help you and watch you succeed. Seek out a therapist who is the right fit for you and start focusing on releasing the emotional scars that are holding you back so you can stop the ripples and take control of your life.

Ways to Turn a Bad Day into a Good Day

Everyone has a bad day, but that doesn't mean you need to go to bed early and feel sorry for yourself. You can turn a terrible day around at any time by following one (or several) of these steps.

Look at old photographs. Go through photographs that show off some of your best days. You might find pictures taken during your last holiday and see yourself laughing. You might put a smile on your face when you run into your friends from high school. You could even find a picture you took yesterday of your pets doing something silly or cute. The key is to focus on the ones that make you smile, laugh, and put you in a lighter mood. If you have a little time to sit and relax, make a scrapbook out of the photos. Even if it's through an online software that only takes you a few minutes, you'll notice that you feel better.

Embrace your negativity. It sounds counterintuitive but accepting the way you're feeling can help you move on from your bad mood faster. The idea is that you allow yourself to say, "It's okay to feel this way, as everyone does" and you come to terms with it. You don't try to ignore it or brush it off because this can make the emotions come back quickly and with a vengeance.

Analyse your thoughts. Why are you feeling this way? What caused your bad mood? How long have you been in this mindset? Did you have a part in it, or does it focus on other people? Ask yourself a series of questions to get a better understanding of how you're feeling and why. Look for solutions in your answers that will help you overcome your negativity so you can start to change your day. But, you want to keep yourself from falling into the trap of self-blame or blaming other people for your mistakes. It's a tricky line to follow, but either one can hold you back from making your day better. If you made mistakes, see what you can do differently to change course the next time and the move forward.

Ask a friend to go on a walk. Take some time to meet up with a friend and go for a walk. It doesn't need to be a long stroll, about 20 to 30 minutes quickly cheers someone up. You can take this time to vent about your frustrations and then focus on the good moments. You might tell each other silly stories to lighten the mood.

Get into beast mode. Put your bad mood energy into a workout. You don't need to overexert yourself by lifting more weight than you should, but you should do what makes you feel good as this will help lift your mood. You might get on the treadmill and run a little faster than normal or find yourself practising your boxing skills.

Realise that bad moments happen. It's important to put your negative mood into perspective. Ask yourself, "Am I having a bad day or was it just a bad moment?" If you recognise that you're letting one moment change the course of your whole day, ask yourself why. Whether that moment went on for a few seconds or a couple of hours, it shouldn't set the mood for your day. There is not one moment within your whole day that can set the mood because it's always up to you. Take time to think about the positives about your day to help change your mindset.

Take a moment to let it go. Sometimes it works better for you if you take a couple of minutes to let go of your negative mood. You're not ignoring it or pushing it away; you're acknowledging that you feel this way but you're not going to let it ruin your whole day. Pledge to yourself that you'll take a couple of deep breaths and release the bad energy from your body. Once you do this, let it go. Don't think about the situation again. If you do, simply let the thought flow out of your head. The key is to not use your energy to feed the bad mood.

Small Ways to Practise Self-Care When You Feel Too Busy

You know you've been there. You feel overworked, overstressed, and know you need to take some quality "me time" but you don't feel right taking a break. You need to make the evening meal for your family, help your children with their homework, play with them, get them ready for bed and help them fall asleep. You also have several house chores you need to finish and want to spend quality time with your partner. Before you go to bed, you need to prepare for the next day by getting everyone's lunches ready.

When do you have time for self-care when you have so much to worry about? You can't take a break to go for a 20-minute walk or watch a Netflix movie. You feel that everything you're allowed to do to focus on your mental and emotional health takes too long.

But it doesn't. In fact, there are many options that don't take long at all. There are also ways that you can easily work self-care into your busy day.

- Take a shower. All you need is a few relaxing minutes to help yourself feel refreshed.
- If you work from home, take time to get dressed and ready for the day. It's easy to stay in your pyjamas and comfy clothes, but it's not what's best for your mental health. Set your alarm clock

for a certain time and treat your work-from-home career like you would if going to an office building.
- Take time away from your phone. If you're working, put your phone on silent or "do not disturb" and let it be. You might even shut off your phone for a few hours during the evening to spend quality time with yourself and your family. Unless you're emergency personnel and need access to your phone, everything else can wait for a few hours.
- Give yourself a bedtime and stick to you. It's easy to find yourself wanting to stay up watching Netflix but it's more important to ensure you get seven to eight hours of sleep every night. Plus, setting a bedtime can help you stay in a routine, which eases your mind.
- Don't be ashamed to cry. It's a regular response to several emotions such as sadness, anger, and frustration. Sometimes letting your eyes water for a period of time can help you feel relaxed and emotionally recharged.
- Take a couple of minutes and go wash your face, especially at night or in the morning. You will feel refreshed and ready to take on the day or find yourself sleeping better. Think of how peaceful a

shower or bath is, washing your face soothes you in the same way.
- Think about something funny and let yourself laugh. Don't worry if people hear or see you laughing, you can always try to explain why you're laughing. You might even make them laugh or smile, which can also make you feel better.

Benefits of Getting a Good Night's Sleep

You live a busy life. It seems that your schedule runs from the time you get up until late into the night. Sometimes you find yourself going to bed four to five hours before your alarm will go off. Other nights you struggle to get to sleep because you're stressed or your mind won't turn off. You might feel that it's better for you to stay up late because you can watch what you want and don't have to worry about your family now sound asleep in their beds.

Unfortunately, lack of sleep is one of the main reasons for declining mental, physical, and emotional health. When you don't get a good night's sleep you can't think clearly, focus, control your emotions, and you're more likely to become physically ill with a cold or flu. To help you realise the importance of a good seven to eight hours of sleep every night, read the benefits below.

Sleep improves your memory. One of the reasons your memory is poor could be because you don't sleep well during the night. While your body rests during night, your brain is busy organising and storing your memories from that day. When you don't get the sleep you need, your brain can't finish its job so it's harder for you to recall your memories.

It improves your physical health. Have you ever wondered why you feel the need to sleep more when you're sick? This is because your body fights back against unwelcomed bacteria and viruses when you're resting.

Sleep helps keep your body balanced. If you feel that your emotions are unbalanced or you're irritable, it could be because you're not getting the right amount of sleep. Your body rests and heals itself when you're in a deep sleep, which regulates your hormones and mood.

You have more motivation. When you sleep well you can concentrate on tasks. You have a higher self-confidence, and this helps your motivation. Take time to remember a day where you barely slept and then think about your progress at work. Compare this to a time where you slept well and how much work you accomplished.

Don't forget about the naps. You might not have cared for naps as a child, but now you probably love them. In fact, you have days where you crave a nap. You might even request to take a nap during your birthday, Mother's Day, or Father's Day. The truth is, you should take a nap as often as you can and need to because sleep makes you smarter. You'll feel refreshed and more attentive, which can give you an added boost of energy for the rest of the day.

Overcoming Your Fears: Facing Anxiety and Phobias

Fear paralyses you. It builds your anxiety so you believe that you can't reach your goals. You worry about what people will think if you make a mistake. You fear what your boss will say when you tell them that you need to extend a deadline for your project.

Fear and anxiety are two words that you probably understand greatly. In my article on *Thought Catalog*, I discuss the differences between the two and offer [6 ways to help you take charge of your fear](). I urge you to visit this article through the link, but also continue reading because there are several ways that you can overcome your fears.

Imagine yourself as unafraid. You are a superhero. Go on, say it to yourself, "I am a superhero." Even though fear and anxiety are a part of life and natural emotions, you don't want to let them control you. Instead, you need to find strategies to control these feelings and one is by visualising yourself as fearless. No matter what situation you're struggling to overcome, close your eyes and imagine yourself doing it. You complete the process without a problem and you don't feel one ounce of fear. Think about how this would make you feel and really hold on to those emotions. They will become a motivation for you when you start your journey.

Give your fear a timeline. It's important that you don't fall into the habit of ignoring your fears. You want to recognise them and then find a way to release them. One step to take is to let yourself be afraid for two to three minutes. Make the conscious effort to tell yourself that your time is starting and then set your alarm so when you hear the tone go off, you release your emotions. Then, it's time to confront your fears.

Use humour. If you're a person that releases negativity through laughter, find something that makes you laugh. You might tell yourself a joke or read a few online. You can even think about the last situation that made you laugh and repay it in your mind. Be creative and think of a way to laugh at the situation that makes you afraid.

Appreciate your courage. It takes a lot of courage to face your fears and this is something you need to appreciate about yourself. You might give yourself a little reward for completing the task or say, "Good job. I am proud of myself for overcoming my fear and making myself stronger.

*"Authenticity is Worth More than a Billion Dollars-
Be authentic. Be yourself not because you have "no other choice,"
but because that is the most amazing person to be.
Authenticity can be defined in many ways,
but the most wonderful thing about it is that you get to
define your own sense of authenticity.
So, allow yourself to be."*
- Amy Reis Williams

Chapter 3:

Awareness

When you think of awareness the first thought to pop into your mind is probably self-awareness. This is a big part of developing your awareness, but it's also only one piece of the puzzle because you need to focus on it externally and internally. In many ways, strengthening your awareness of your environment, self, and other people helps you improve various areas of your life. For example, understanding and noticing your emotions helps you feel empathy toward other people. You might not directly understand how they are feeling but you do know how the emotion feels and this helps you understand their point of view. It helps build connections in your relationships, acquaintances, and the world around you.

The Five Stages of Awareness Mastery

Developing awareness is a gradual process that focuses on five main stages. You're already aware of certain parts of your personality and environment. For example, you know when you're tired, hungry, and when you feel particular emotions. You'll build on this foundation throughout the rest of your life.

Have you ever heard the phrase "knowledge is power?" It means that the more you know, the more power you'll have in your life. There is truth to this saying but it's not the whole truth. There are a couple of steps that it's missing between "knowledge" and "power." Awareness is one step, coming after knowledge. From awareness you move to control and then power. Therefore, to get to power you need to master awareness.

The first stage is feeling clueless. No matter how much you don't want to admit it, there's been times where you didn't know what you were doing. You might have looked to a classmate's paper to see if they understood or went back to reread the directions, a bit more slowly. It's a frustrating time and one people don't like talking about. But without the lost feeling you won't reach awareness mastery.

One reason for this stage is because your frontal cortex develops last. In fact, it doesn't mature until your 20s. This means that children and young adults don't receive its full benefits, which can cause them to feel clueless when it comes to learning something new. They have more trouble making decisions, thinking rationally, expressing their personality, and moderating social behaviour. When you mix this with the second reason, which is an educational system that doesn't cater to the best way they learn on an individual basis, you meet a group of people who choose less action when they need to make decisions. They also feel they lack power because they don't always understand what their elders are trying to teach them. This leads them to lose self-confidence, followed by emotional and psychological problems.

You can overcome this first stage by growing older, but you also need to focus on your emotional and psychological awareness at the same time. Understand your limitations during this period and have patience when it comes to learning. If you're older than 25 and still struggling, it's time to dive into meditation, becoming more motivated, improving social skills, and working out.

The second stage is knowing yourself. You need to become conscious to become aware and understand yourself. You explore why you feel and think certain ways. For example, if you become aware of a negative thought pattern, why? Does it stem from your childhood? Did it start in your adult years? Ask yourself a number of questions to get an understanding of who you are and why you became this person.

At this stage, you don't want to focus on how you need to act so you belong to a certain group. For example, don't act how your friends act. This isn't taking the step to understanding yourself, it's learning how to act like someone else. You need to focus on *you*. Even when you find the dark side of your personality, get to know it. Learn why this side of you exists. Remember, it's not a negative factor to have a dark side because everyone does. It's all a part of being human. Your actions determine what type of person you are.

Once you have an understanding of you, it's time to move to the third stage: social patterns. This is a complex stage because there are a lot of strands that you need to weave together to get the best understanding. You start looking at the way society operates when you are a child. So, what type of environment you grew up in will have an effect in your adult years. It will cause you to believe certain myths or rumours and make you turn away from other truths. The key is to keep your mind and heart open; follow your instincts as this will guide you to the real truth of society.

You will focus on three parts within this step, which are empathy, power dynamics, and persuasion or influence. Empathy is when you start to connect with another human through emotions. Power dynamics is understanding the sophisticated set of tools. You know that to maintain order you need to have a system, and you support it. At the same time, you're not afraid to ask questions and look for the truth. Persuasion and influence help us follow the laws. They give us a bit of stability so we feel safe and can continue to grow within ourselves.

The fourth stage is when you feel like you're going crazy. You'll come to a point where you realise that you're not the same person you were before, and this becomes strange to you. You might feel like you wasted time learning who you were in stage two but in reality, you grew beyond your knowledge. Your conscious mind became stronger as it started to notice pieces of your unconscious mind that moved over to your awareness.

One way to handle this stage is to go with the flow and don't stop your emotional and psychological development. Your mind isn't designed for this stage, so it can catch you off-guard and even make you feel afraid of continuing the process. Don't fight it, don't get mad, and don't get scared. Instead, be gentle with yourself and move through the process gradually. Another important tip is to talk to yourself. You can talk to your friends, family, and even a therapist as they can help you develop in this stage, but self-talk is just as important.

Finally, you'll reach the stage of accepting human nature and controlling your narrative. You will understand that chaos and emergencies happen. There is nothing you can do to stop this because it's beyond your control. What is in your control is how you react to these situations. You'll focus on how you react to your emotions and further develop into your self-awareness, its levels, mindfulness, and emotional intelligence.

The Levels of Self-Awareness

Self-awareness doesn't just involve five stages, but it also has three separate levels: what you're doing, how you feel about it, and learning what you don't know about yourself. This last level is considered the hardest part but is essential for your growth. These levels will work alongside the stages, which can become a negative or positive. For instance, you might feel it's negative during the time that you believe you're losing your mind, or you don't understand what is happening. You might feel like they're working positively together when you're feeling empathy toward another person or learning how to take control.

What are you doing? Stop whatever you're doing and take yourself off of autopilot so you can become mindful of your emotions, thoughts, and actions. If you're making dinner, think about the steps that you're doing to prepare the dinner. How do you grab your plates? How do you set the table? How many times do you chew each bite of your food? Make sure you take time out of your day to get away from your devices, such as your computer, phone, and television. Focus on the present moment and notice your body's sensations. How does the plate feel in your hand? How does it feel to stir the meal?

How do you feel? Not only should you focus on how it feels when you go through your motions, but also how you generally feel. Sit down without any distractions and dig deep within your heart and soul. Take time to figure out your true emotions right now. You might be surprised to learn that you feel a little blue, bored, or angry at where your life is at the moment. Like most people, you easily bottle up your negative emotions so you can tell yourself you're happy or excited for the next phase of your life without realizing that you're a little sad or scared.

What can you do about the way you're feeling? Now it's the hard part. You need to think about what you can do to change the way you're feeling or your thoughts. For example, if you're feeling sad, why? Ask yourself what factors have led to this emotion and be truthful with yourself. Sometimes the truth hurts, and this makes us want to cover it up, but you need to open yourself up. This is the only way you can start to become more aware of yourself, your environment, and other people.

Importance of Mindfulness

When you're mindfully aware, you are tuned in to what's going on in the present moment. You're not focused on your mistakes of the past and you're not worried about the future. You are concerned with what is happening to you in this very second. You're analysing your thoughts and feelings and how they connect to what is happening around you.

Strengthening your mindfulness is an area in your life you need to practise every day. There are many strategies that can help change your mindset from mindlessness, which is when you're daydreaming and not directly focused on your thoughts or environment, to mindfulness.

If you practise yoga, you can observe the way your body feels with every pose. Take a moment to notice how you start, your process during the exercising, and then how you finish. How does your body feel throughout the process? Do you start to feel more relaxed? Ask yourself a variety of questions to help stay in the moment.

Take time for yourself. Find a place where you can relax in silence and pay attention to your thoughts. You can also note the sounds you hear, aroma, and anything else about your environment. Be mindful about everything that is happening internally and externally.

Notice everything that's a part of the conversation, such as accents, tone of voice, and what they are saying. Don't let your mind wander to a different conversation in your head or to a daydream. Let your mind stay focused on what is going on around you and recognise how much you enjoy the moment.

Awareness of Your Mental Health

Mental health includes your psychological, emotional, and social well-being. It's one of the most important pieces of you because it follows you from your early childhood years and throughout your adulthood. It helps you make decisions, guides you on how to act, and influences your mindset. When you take care of yourself, you get the most out of life. You feel more motivated to reach your goals and your highest self.

One of the first steps to take is talking about your emotions. It's not a sign of weakness; it's a sign of strength and taking control of your mental health. Talking gives you an avenue to cope with what's on your mind. For example, instead of telling your partner, "nothing" when asked what's wrong, open up and tell them how you feel. Even if you don't exactly know what is bothering you, let them know that you're feeling blue or deep in thought.

Another tip is to stay in the present. You want to follow the rules of mindfulness so you can remain aware of your thoughts, behaviours, and understand yourself. When you start to feel certain emotions, such as anger or sadness, you can analyse the situation and take note of any triggers that caused your feelings.

You want to think positively. Several psychological studies prove focusing on positive thoughts helps increase your self-confidence. You start to tell yourself "I will do this" instead of "I think I can." You need to focus on thoughts that are helpful and lift your spirits over the negativity that enters your mind.

Looking after your mental health branches out to your environment. To create a positive mindset, you need to fill your world with positivity. This isn't easy when other people are struggling or bringing in the negativity. Take a moment to notice which friends and family members support your healthy thoughts and lifestyle so you can turn your attention onto them. Spend time with them as they will help your mental health blossom like a beautiful flower.

When you feel overwhelmed by the world around you, take a time out. Find a place you can go where peace can follow. Take time to relax and unwind so you can begin to focus on what's important for your mindset. One of the most important keys to learning about yourself is to put your mental health first.

Reaching Your Emotional Intelligence

Once you reach self-awareness you can start to focus on emotional intelligence. This is when you become aware of your emotions. You learn how to identify them and their triggers so you can focus on your reactions.

You have many skills that will help you reach your emotional intelligence. You can start by continuing to become more self-aware. The more you notice your thoughts, feelings, and reactions the easier it is to learn how to control them.

One step you can take to strengthen this piece of you is to channel your emotions thoroughly. This goes beyond learning about your emotions. It brings you to a whole other level of how you react to them internally and externally. Treat your emotions as signals that alert you to pay attention to what is happening to you or around you. Channelling allows you to control your actions to the best of your abilities, so you don't make decisions on how you feel. Instead, you think rationally about the situation and make the best choice for you and everyone else involved.

Once you've spent time on channelling and becoming more aware of your emotions, turn this attention to other people. Strengthen your empathy as this will allow you to further reach your emotional intelligence. Empathy doesn't mean that you understand the way they are feeling. It means that you accept their emotions and who they are.

You also need to bring value into your emotions. Your energy is always directed toward your values, which creates your emotions. Without connecting your values your emotional intelligence won't reach its highest level and you won't live the life you truly want.

Signs Your Self-Confidence is Low and How to Start Loving Yourself

Self-confidence is a characteristic that most people need to improve in themselves. It's an important piece of your life that describes how you feel about your abilities. When you have high confidence, you know that you can accomplish anything you set your mind to. Even if you fail, you know that it's okay to try again because you will succeed eventually. You also know how to take your mistakes and learn from them. When you have low self-confidence, you struggle to make it through the work day. You might think about dropping out of school or drop out because you don't believe you're smart enough. You might jump from job to job because you don't think you're good enough for any position.

Because your confidence helps strengthen your self-esteem and mindset, you need to understand when it's low so you can focus on improving it and yourself. Here are a few signs that prove your self-confidence is low so you can overcome this challenge through self-love.

- Do you often go through dozens of filters to try to hide your face when you take a selfie? You might take several different pictures and then go through them all dozens of times to try to find the right one to post on social media.
- When you meet someone new on the street do you immediately start to like them and wish you could be more like them? You think about how perfect their hair is or how they look like someone who has a nice home and is financially stable.
- You take the blame in every situation or find yourself saying "I'm sorry" often.
- Even when you do well on a project, you still belittle yourself or think about everything you did wrong.
- You don't look people in the eye when you're conversing.
- You care about how many people like your posts on social media. If you don't receive likes, you think it's a stupid post and might take it down because you're embarrassed about it.
- When someone gives you a compliment you don't believe them or you're not sure how to handle it. For example, you might smile and

giggle or you say "thank you" just because you know it's the polite response.
- You struggle with your posture and usually walk hunched over.
- When you write comments on social media you worry about what other people will say and might delete it.
- You expect to do the worst, even if you enjoy the task and think that you might be good at it. For instance, you believe that someone else would do it better or that you're not the right person for the project.

If you relate to some of the bullet points, it's time to practise self-love. You can do this by following some of these steps:

- Every morning when you wake up, look in the mirror, and say something positive about yourself. It could be something that you did the

day before or a characteristic, such as compassion, that you feel strongly about.
- Spend your time with people who encourage you to do your best. They will also support you when you make a mistake or fail.
- Do something that makes you smile.
- Take time to celebrate your wins. It doesn't matter how small they are.
- Try something new by stepping outside of your comfort zone so you know what you can accomplish.
- Continue to push yourself to learn something new and discover all of your talents and skills.
- Embrace your differences because they're what make you special.
- Do you best to always treat other people with respect and compassion. When you treat

someone well, you start to feel better about yourself.

Focus on letting go of your need for approval by other people. Learn to find the approval you desire within yourself.

It's Time to Stop Doubting Yourself

Self-doubt is that voice that holds you back from what you want to accomplish in your life. It might tell you that you can't do something or that you're not strong enough. It makes it harder to find your motivation and grab onto opportunities that are right in front of you.

You don't want to get rid of all your self-doubt because it can help you when making the right decisions or tell you when an idea is bad. But you don't want to let it control your life. You can't allow it to take over your good ideas, motivation, self-love, and confidence. You need to learn how to manage it, so you know when it's helpful and when it's pulling you back. To ensure that your doubt isn't stopping you from moving forward, follow the tips below.

First, you want to realise that having a little doubt is okay, so embrace it as part of being a human. Recognise that everyone has this little doubt voice in their head and that it's okay to hear it. The key is you want to understand when it's helping you and when it's harming you. You need to stop beating yourself up when you make a mistake. You also need to stop beating yourself up for beating yourself up. You're human so remember that mistakes and failures are a part of life. Analyse the situation so you know what you can learn from it, pick up any pieces, and move forward.

Second, don't spend a lot of time trying to come up with the perfect decisions. You're not moulded to ensure that you take the right step every time. Take time to reflect on the choices you have and then make the one you feel is the best. If it's not, correct it along the way.

Third, face one fear daily. Make it a mission to think about a fear that you have and want to overcome. It could be as small as calling someone on the phone without spending five minutes questioning if you should call now or later. It might also be a bigger fear such as learning how to drive. Whatever you want to do, write it down and then take time to do it. While you can't face every fear in one day as some will take a few days, such as learning how to drive, you can make it a goal and work towards it every day until you reach your destination.

Fourth, help yourself remember the positive parts of your life. It's easier to remember the bad events or how people hurt you, but this won't manage your doubt. In fact, it adds to it. Reflect on your life with the understanding that you will acknowledge negative memories but will not spend time on them. You will only focus on the good memories. To help, you can think of moments that make you smile. Once you start thinking on the bright side, you'll find more memories floating into your mind. You can also write them down so when you need a boost, you have a place to go.

Finally, sometimes what people say about you is a reflection of themselves. It's important to take what some people say with a grain of salt. You might want to be respectful and let them know that you appreciate their opinion but then don't take it to heart. Sometimes other people are disrespectful or verbally lash out because they're having a bad day, or they feel worthless and want you to feel the same way. Understand that sometimes people aren't thinking clearly or don't have a positive mindset. One step to handle these difficult moments is to forgive them and then continue being you.

Benefits That Prove It's Good to Cry

Crying is a natural response to various emotions and irritants such as wind and smoke. Depending on how sensitive you are, will affect how often you cry. For example, someone who is highly sensitive or empathic cries easily. Many people feel that it's embarrassing to cry in front of other people, but it actually shows strength and that you wear your heart on your sleeve. Furthermore, whether you cry alone or with others, there are benefits that prove crying is a positive response for your overall health.

Crying helps relieve pain. One of the reasons people cry is because they're in pain, whether it's physical or emotional. For example, you slide down the stairs and immediately start crying over the pain you feel in your ankle. You might also cry at the news of a loved one's death or the loss of your job. According to research, tears release oxytocin and endorphins that help you self-soothe during a difficult time.

Relieve stress. You break down and cry when you start to feel stressed and overwhelmed. When you stop crying, you realise that you feel better. Even if you still feel some stress, it's not as heavy as it was before. This is because tears contain chemicals and stress hormones. Therefore, crying is literally like releasing some of the stress you feel inside of your body.

Crying as its own soothing effect. A 2014 study proved that crying helps people feel more relaxed because it activates the parasympathetic nervous system (Burgess, 2017). When people self-soothe, they not only calm themselves but also destress and manage their emotions better.

Improves your mood. Think back to the last time you cried. It might have been over a movie, death of a pet, or life stress. Try to remember how you felt before the tears started flowing and how you felt after. If memory serves you correctly, you'll recognise that you felt better after you released tears. This is because your mood improves after you cry, whether it's just a few tears or you spend minutes bawling. The trick here is when you're sobbing, you take in quick breaths of cold air, which helps lower the temperature of your brain. You make your body feel better with a cooler brain and this helps regulate your emotions.

It brings support. When you cry in front of other people, you'll find support. It's not always easy to ask people to help you through difficult times, but they'll always do their best when they know that you need them. Crying is an honest human reaction that lets people know how you're truly feeling, so they can be there to lend a hand.

Your emotions become balanced. Crying happens with nearly every emotion because it's a natural reaction when you feel one way too strongly. For instance, you cry when you're happy and you don't know how to express your gratitude. You cry when you're sad and grieving. It's your body's way to recover from a strong emotion.

Hopefully after reading these benefits you feel more comfortable crying in front of other people. Don't worry about how you look because it's a natural reaction and you're allowing your body and mind to heal.

Tips to Help You Manage a Healthier Eating Lifestyle

You've probably tried more than one diet in your lifetime for whatever reason. You live in a world where there are so many diets that it's hard to know which one is best for you. The thought of losing a few kilograms in an attempt to decrease your chances of heart disease causes people to want a healthier lifestyle, especially when it comes to their meals. It's not easy to follow a diet, no matter how long you've been on one, because there are so many convenient places to grab a quick lunch. Of course, your busy days don't help.

The key to maintaining a healthier eating lifestyle isn't just following a diet. There are a lot of factors that contribute, such as a regular sleep schedule, limiting stress, and motivation.

Turn your diet into a choice. Sometimes you struggle with your diet because you feel forced to take it on. It's easier to follow a lifestyle change when you believe that it's your choice. Before you start the diet, make a plan to sit down and consciously make the decision to start dieting. You can do this by setting a start date and choosing your own diet.

Choose water. One of the biggest tips experts will tell you when it comes to losing weight and keeping yourself healthy is to drink more water. You should drink at least eight glasses of water every day, but if you also have a habit of picking up sugary drinks it's time to choose refreshing water instead.

Cut out the mayo. If you love mayonnaise, you need to pick a date where you say goodbye to it. Instead, you want to choose mustard for your sandwiches. One reason you want to cut out mayo-based products is because they're the worst condiment to choose. They're high in bad fats and calories, which can cause you to gain weight and contribute to heart disease and other health issues.

Switch to fat-free milk. If you buy standard milk, you might consider switching to fat-free milk. While standard milk is a great drink and can help you maintain your bone health, it contains saturated fats and calories. The lower fat content, the less calories. If you already drink fat-free milk, you're well on the road to maintaining a healthier lifestyle!

Be choosy about your nighttime snacking. How often and late do you snack at night? Snacking at night is a leading cause to weight gain because you have a harder time burning the calories. Plus, it's easier to choose unhealthy snacks before bed. If you need to settle your stomach to sleep because you feel like you're starving, grab a glass of milk or water. But, the best step to take is to close down the kitchen at a certain hour. Don't allow yourself to eat anything about three hours before you go to bed.

Eat several small meals during the day. If it's doable with your family, eat several small meals during the day. For example, you can start your day at 7:30 a.m. with an egg and slice of whole wheat toast. Three hours later, you can eat fruit, such as an apple or orange. At 1:00 p.m. you can have one of your main meals, such as a pasta bowl. You can have another lighter meal, such as yogurt and rice cakes at 3:30 p.m. and then a salad at 6:30.

As a bonus, here is a recipe for a yummy Mixed Berries Smoothie Bowl.

Prep time: 5 minutes

Servings: 1

Smoothie bowl ingredients:

- 100 g ripe frozen banana
- 160 g frozen mixed berries
- 30-45 ml almond or coconut milk
- 1 scoop vanilla or plain protein powder

Ingredients for topping:

- 12 g chia seeds
- 5 g shredded unsweetened coconut
- 10 g hemp seeds
- Your favourite chopped fruit (optional)
- Granola (optional)

Directions:

1. Combine the banana and berries into a blender and mix on low until tiny bits remain.
2. Add in the milk and protein powder. Blend on low until you have a smooth consistency.
3. Scoop into a bowl and top with hemp seeds, unsweetened coconut, chia seeds, fruit, granola,

or any other nutritious ingredients that make your mouth water.
4. It's best to eat fresh, but you can keep any leftovers in the freezer for seven to 10 days.

"What you get by achieving your goals is not as important as what you become by achieving your goals."
- Zig Ziglar (Picard, 2018)

Chapter 4:

Breathe

Take a deep breath to help you relax. How many times a day do you stop and focus on your breathing? You probably rarely focus on your regular breathing except when you're told by the doctor to "take a deep breath" during an exam or maybe you spontaneously have the urge to pay a bit more attention. However, like most people, you probably go through the motions quickly. You don't stop and think about how your lungs are filled with clean, fresh air and how it's released back into the world.

This time, I want you to take another deep breath but go slow. You can close your eyes and feel your lungs when you breathe in. Notice how they fill with the cool air. Take note of how your body feels. If you kept your eyes open, did you watch your chest move up? When you think of your lungs, do they feel a little colder than before because of the air?

Now, focus on releasing your breath. Breathe out and notice the senses of your body again. What differences do you pick up on? Are there any similarities?

A deep breath is powerful. It can help you clear your mind and keep you focused on a task. It can also help you release tension. Through these essays, you'll realise the importance of allowing a break, noticing the beauty around you, and taking a breath.

Don't Rush Through Your Life, Notice the Beauty

You know the importance of goals and setting deadlines. They help keep you on track and fulfil your life's mission. You set goals that only take a few days and others that take years. You've learned it's crucial to think of where you'll be in five or ten years from now.

The trouble comes when the stress starts. You set goals and start to panic, wondering if you can accomplish them and how. You ask yourself why you would set goals that you can't achieve. It can cause you to cross out dreams, leaving you feel like you've failed. From there, your confidence and self-esteem can dwindle down, affecting the rest of your goals. It can also cause you to lose faith in yourself.

The trouble comes when you try to manifest what you want as quickly as possible. You don't set realistic steps for your goals because you want the ideal job NOW or the bigger house NOW. You want to be financially stable NOW.

The turning point in your life comes when you realise that beauty takes time. Creating the life you want, healing from your past, and reaching your goals isn't something that you can manifest instantly. You want to have patience for it and allow it to come to you through the steps you take to create your wonderful life.

The key is to care more about climbing the mountain than reaching the top. You need to focus on your progress and look back at it every step of the way. You're focused on the top because as you climb, you're told not to look down, but this is exactly what you should do. You want to stop and take a look back at what you've accomplished so you know exactly where you're heading.

Stop rushing the timing of your life because you don't need to manifest everything you want immediately. You'll find more beauty on the way as you pace yourself along the path. You can even take time to stop and smell the flowers, as this helps heal your heart and soul. Give your mind a rest when you feel that you're stressed or overworked.

Stop rushing so you can take time to enjoy the path you've walked and the direction you're taking in life. Take a deep breath, close your eyes, smile, look up to the sky, and allow the calm air to flow around you. Take pride in the work you've accomplished because it proves that you're getting somewhere.

It's Better to Breathe Than to Plan

You probably heard about the importance of planning for your day, a business, or what you want to do in five years. Since you can remember, you've focused on making plans for your life, whether it's to go out with your friends or develop your career path. While you want to establish goals and this requires planning, you also need to understand that there is no plan. There's not a big plan for your life. Even if you have planned out your life, it's not written in stone. It will change over time.

The truth is your brain isn't wired to plan for the future, especially long-term. It's also not meant to work according to a schedule. Your brain tends to go with the flow, especially when it comes to your thoughts. It's more focused on your senses and what you're learning. Your mind is focused on gathering as much information as possible and sorting it into long-term or short-term memory.

Yes, you can plan out your day but how often does it go exactly as scheduled? Take a moment to think about what you write down in your planner and how well you can stick to it. What happens when that meeting goes a few minutes longer or the school calls to tell you to pick up your sick child? When you make plans and they don't go as scheduled you start to feel negatively. You might feel frustrated that your friend cancelled plans or stressed because you have to take a day off of work. How will you catch up on your project? When will you make up the hours? Will you be able to afford to pay your bills?

Planning makes us less flexible to life. It makes us feel unorganized when emergencies happen or you need to make abrupt changes. This causes you to struggle emotionally and mentally.

It's okay to take time to make plans, lists, and do what you need to do so you feel organized and less stressed, but you also need to ensure that you take time to breathe. You need to allow yourself to go with the flow of life, be flexible, and understand that true plans don't exist.

Important Steps of Mindfulness Meditation

When it comes to setting up your meditation area you need to follow your heart. If you want to listen to calming music or use guided meditation on YouTube, incorporate this into your meditation. You might also light candles or leave a window open just a crack for some fresh air. Once you sit down in your area, notice the comfort and peace you receive from the environment. Then, you can start focusing on the common steps to practise mindfulness meditation.

1. Find a comfortable position in your calm and quiet area to lay down. Take a deep breath and allow your body to form with the foundation of the couch, bed, chair, or ground.
2. Take another deep breath and close your eyes. Become aware of the sounds around you. Let them be as you start to relax your body into the foundation. Take another deep and slow breath, inhaling through your nose and exhaling out of your mouth.
3. Continue to focus on your deep breaths. Your mind is starting to let go of all the concerns it had.
4. Place one hand on your chest and the other on your stomach. Breathe in through your nose and

feel the movements of your body. Notice how your stomach and chest lift up as you fill your lungs with air. Hold your breath for a couple of seconds before you exhale out your mouth, carrying your concerns away.

5. Return to your normal breathing. Don't control your breaths but allow them to fall into their natural rhythm. You'll continue to feel your body sink into the foundation as your muscles relax. Now, start counting each breath you take. Begin with one and go up to ten, then start back at one.

6. Be gentle with your wandering mind. Bring your focus back to your breaths and continue to count.

7. In the first few minutes of meditation, you'll start to become absorbed in your breath. You'll find it easier to bring yourself back to counting. It's at this time you'll start focusing on your thoughts, beginning with the most important one to come to your mind. Accept each thought and then let it drift from your meditative state, making way for a new thought. Repeat this process without focusing too much attention on any one reflection over another. Each time you catch yourself becoming too involved in one idea or emotion, bring yourself back to your breathing.

8. After a few minutes you can start to focus on your breathing again. Start bringing yourself out

of your meditative state slowly. Breathe in and out naturally for a few minutes and then focus on the sensations your body feels. It might be the way your stomach expands with each breath or the way your clothes feel on your skin. Listen to the noises happening around you to help bring your mind back into your environment. Once you're ready, open your eyes and look around your area. Wiggle your fingers and toes to get your body moving again.

Always Remember to Breathe

Remind yourself to breathe when you feel your anxiety creep up on you. Close your eyes, take a deep breath in through your nose. Fill your lungs up with air and hold it there for a couple of seconds. Then, slowly release your breath through your mouth. Feel the sensations of your body as your lungs deflate with air. Notice the calmness that starts to wash over you.

If you need to, take a few more deep breaths before you focus on the next phase in your day. Don't rush through the breaths, take your time. Everything you feel like you need to accomplish in that moment will get done at the right time. Now, is the time to focus on *you* and your mental health.

Remind yourself to breathe when you can't stop crying. When you feel like your chest is tight and you don't know if you can breathe.

Breathe deeply and slowly when you feel like your mind is cluttered with thoughts. Place your hand on your chest and feel its sensations when you take a deep breath in and then out. Continue to hold your hand there as you feel your heartbeats' rhythm becoming calmer.

Remember to breathe when you feel like giving up and the walls are closing in around you.

Stop, close your eyes and take a few slow breaths when you feel that no one cares about you. When you worry that you're not good enough and won't reach your full potential.

You might not even know why you feel the way that you do. You just have so many emotions that are overwhelming. You try to sort them out, but it only makes it worse. Realise that it's okay to feel you're lost in the world and can't understand why you are here. Breathe and know that you have a purpose.

You might feel that there is no more love within you. I know that you feel exhausted and don't know how you will carry on. You no longer recognise who you are or who you want to become. It's okay to wait for your healing to come. Take it one breath at the time.

Release Yourself From Past Hurt and Trauma

It's easy to let your past hurt and trauma hold you hostage. These are the ghosts that come to you at night when you're trying to sleep or sneak up on you during the day when you're trying to complete a project. They don't warn you that they're coming, but you can feel them creep into your brain as the event starts to replay in your mind. You might feel the same emotions you felt in that moment. They make you question your abilities and worry about the future. You might feel ashamed or guilty for what happened, even though you had no control over it.

These burdens that you carry are a heavy weight on your mind and body. The reality is you can't change what happened, but you can change how you react now and how it affects your future. It's time to take control of your past trauma and pain so you can begin to let it go. It's time to stand up for yourself. You need to stop focusing on trying to ensure that everyone else is happy and make sure the person you see every day in the mirror is happy.

Don't feel like you need to stop the rattling alone. There are many people who are willing to help you, from your friends to a therapist. To support you along your path, here are a few ways to help you release:

Change your interpretation of the past. No, you can't change the actions from the past, but you can change how you interpret it. Think about it this way—two people can read the same story and come up with a different meaning. The same goes with your past. For example, you might think that classmates didn't like you but come to realise they felt intimidated by you because of your good grades, looks, or skills.

When you start to change your view, you need to ask yourself a few questions. Start by going back and thinking about what happened. Next, ask yourself, "What evidence do I have that helps me come to my understanding?" Then, focus on any assumptions that you have. From there you want to look at any other explanations that you haven't thought about. You can do this by thinking about how your friends or family would interpret the situation. Finally, ask yourself, "What is the healthiest way to look at this event?"

Remember you've grown. Even if your pain comes from a situation that occurred a year ago, you're not the same person. You've changed over the course of the year or many years. You've learned new things. You might have a change in beliefs and values. You might have more self-esteem or confidence. You could also be a more compassionate person than you were before. There are many avenues for growth in your life every day. Don't hang on to something that happened because of who you were before.

Don't avoid it. No one wants to deal with negativity, especially when it's traumatic. But, one of the best ways to overcome it is to look it in the eyes, let it go, and move on. Take the lessons you learned from the situation and grow from it.

Have a conversation with yourself. Use this time to connect with yourself by asking when and how you should release the past. You can do this by following "The Sedona Method" which helps you answer three main questions:

1. Can I release this?
2. Would I release this?
3. If so, when will I release this?

They're simple questions but can be difficult to answer, so take your time. You're not in a rush to get them answered or to let go. You're going through a process to help you advance into your future.

One of the most important takeaway points is that releasing trauma and pain is not easy. It doesn't matter how long you've been a prisoner of it. You'll find that you feel like you're making progress and then start thinking about the past moment again. When this happens, don't feel like you're taking two steps back.

Instead, look at why the memory creeped into your mind. Notice if there are any triggers that caused it and what you can do to help yourself reach the top of the mountain.

Here Are 10 Reminders to Help You When You're Struggling to Better Yourself

1. No one is perfect. The people that you see on your social media feed that seem to have their life in perfect order, face their own struggles. Don't hold yourself to an unrealistic standard because of what you see on Twitter or Facebook. All you're seeing is a segment of their life.
2. Remember that you're trying to better yourself and this is something that many people don't take time to do. You're taking a great step in your life to try to reach the highest peak. You're overcoming obstacles that other people turn away from. Be proud of the path you're on and know you're going in the right direction.
3. Don't be afraid to take a break. Sit down on the couch and binge-watch Netflix for a day. Go out for a walk and spend time outdoors without worrying about the need to pay bills, household

tasks, taking care of other people, or anything else. You deserve to take time away from the stresses of life so you can keep the peace in your mind.
4. Remember what and who you can control. It's easy to feel like you need to control everything around you to find peace, but you know that it's not possible. When you start to feel that your life is cycling out of control, look in the mirror and remind yourself that the only person you can control is *you*. You're in charge of how you act toward situations and what you say to other people.
5. Take time to breathe. When you feel overwhelmed, take a few deep and slow breaths. You might find that you only need to breathe deeply once before you start to feel better. Other times you might need to take a couple of minutes. Don't worry about the amount of time, focus on slowly breathing in through your nose and releasing the air through your mouth.
6. Change is a difficult process. Even when you become comfortable with it, you still might find yourself struggling for different reasons. You may need to change your daily routine or your diet. You might need to make changes to your work schedule so you can ensure you're home with your children. You need to be patient when

it comes to making adjustments, so you don't become overwhelmed.

7. Breaking a bad habit takes time. It's believed that you need at least 21 days to create a new habit. It's also believed that you can easily fall back into a bad habit months later because they're so hard to break. It's challenging to stay away from something you loved to do for so long. You'll find yourself dealing with a couple of setbacks during the process, and that's okay. Don't lose your faith and don't give up.

8. Remind yourself that you're doing great. Sometimes all you need is a little compliment, even from yourself, to get your motivation going. Look in the mirror and say how proud you are of yourself. If you keep a journal, read through the last few months or days and recognize your progress.

9. You're not a bad person. Just because you made a mistake or you need to work on parts of your personality that you consider negative, such as your mindset, it doesn't mean that you're not a good person. You're a wonderful person who deserves the best in life. Tell yourself this every day so you remember how amazing you are.

10. Don't be hard on yourself. You are your worst critic, but this doesn't mean that you should belittle yourself. Use your inner critical voice to

give yourself constructive criticism to better your life. You need to be gentle when you talk about what you need to work on. Speak to yourself like you would your best friend who is struggling.

Ways to Help You Cope With Anxiety Right Now

Anxiety is a word that can cause people to feel stressed just reading it. It's a cycle that can keep you from raising your self-esteem and achieving your full potential. While it's true that having a little anxiety can keep you on track and motivated, it usually builds into a mental disorder that we struggle to manage. In fact, anxiety disorder affects 1 in 4 New Zealanders and approximately 15% of the population at one time (Health Navigator, 2019).

There are a lot of coping strategies for anxiety, but some of them take time that you feel like you don't have. Sometimes your anxiety is so strong that it causes your mind and body to feel like it's paralysed. It's in these moments that you need to follow certain steps to help yourself cope so you can find a way to calm your anxiety and seek the help you need to overcome the disorder.

It's important to note that if you're having a panic attack, you might need to take different measures to find a calmer state. Many people will start to hold something physical or look around the room and focus on what's present to help their anxiety start to calm down. Then, they'll turn their attention to taking slow, deep breaths.

You should also note that some of these tips might work better for you than others. Follow your senses and instincts when it comes to what works for you.

Realise that your body's natural reaction to stress is anxiety. It's normal to feel worried when you're starting a new job, project, or giving a presentation. How many times did you feel nervous and excited before starting your first day back at school? Stress is a part of life, which makes anxiety normal. Sometimes you can help manage it by understanding that everyone feels this way from time to time.

Pause and focus on your breathing. Even though all you can do is think about your current situation, you need to remember that it doesn't shape your day, thought pattern, or your life. It's not easy to take yourself out of a stressful situation, but many people feel better after closing their eyes and taking a few deep, slow breaths. They feel that their thoughts become clearer and they can continue to focus on calming their heart rate, anxiety, or continuing on their project. Another technique to use in this step is to count to ten. Sometimes counting first helps you focus on your breathing.

Tell yourself that you're okay. No matter what you're going through, there is a light at the end of the tunnel. If you ever heard your parents tell you, "This too shall pass" now is the perfect time to remind yourself. You might not directly feel this way in the moment, but when you start saying this out loud, you'll become more open to it as a fact. Another strategy to use at this point is to think about all the times that you felt this way and made it through.

Remind yourself all you can do is your best. You might struggle with anxiety at the moment because you're putting too much pressure on yourself. You feel that your project needs to be perfect when, in fact, nothing is perfect.

Start to understand your triggers. Anxiety comes about from certain triggers, such as public speaking, driving on winter roads, or being told your boss wants to talk to you. Take time to ask yourself why your anxiety started or why you feel that it's out of control. It might help to write down what happened so you can analyse the situation or compare it to other times you've felt nervous or scared.

Use aromatherapy. Sometimes all you need to do is light a candle, use incense, or a diffuser to get the smell of lavender or sandalwood in your home or office. There are several aromas that people find calming, and they're known to help people feel more relaxed. While the scientific research is inconclusive, many psychologists believe that certain smells activate a specific part of your brain that helps you control stress and anxiety.

Help Yourself Heal From a Narcissistic Relationship

Get over it. How do you get over abuse? How do you learn to overcome the effect from a narcissistic relationship? Narcissism is a psychological disorder where someone has an inflated sense of self-worth. They truly believe that they are better than everyone else and use manipulative tactics to make people feel beneath them. They lack empathy and don't have the natural ability to understand that their actions are wrong. They don't see how what they say or do hurts someone else.

If you've been through a narcissistic relationship (or battling one), you know that it's a type of abuse that's different from other types. You can't prove to someone that you're dealing with this type of abuse because it's emotional and mental. The main way you know is because of how you feel, what you think about yourself, and you've learned the signs.

You believed that your partner was the most amazing person you ever met. They made you feel like the most important person. They gave you gifts, supported you, helped your self-esteem grow and then, gradually, they tore it all down. You come to feel that they ripped your heart out and left it on the ground, beating all alone.

No matter where you are in the healing stage, it's important to use a variety of strategies to help you overcome the abuse. It's time for you to take control of your life and here are some ways to help you.

Acknowledge and accept the abuse. It's a tough step to realise that you allowed someone to treat you a certain way. It's this thought that pushes many people into a deep depression, but it's important to do your best not to focus on it. You want to acknowledge and accept that it happened. It was a part of your life; your partner treated you a certain way, and now you need to overcome it. You will blame yourself. It's part of the process, but you can't let blame or guilt control your life. Don't let it stop you from healing and reaching happiness and your full potential.

Challenge your false beliefs. Narcissists make you believe in a false reality. For example, they will tell you something, and then when you say something to them about it, they'll twist your reality. They might tell you that they never said that or say it's something that you said, instead. They also start to make you believe certain characteristics about yourself that aren't true, such as any abuse is your fault or you're a bad person. Take time to write down all of your negative beliefs and challenge them. Tell yourself what they said was wrong and why. For instance, you're not a bad person because you have love in your heart. You don't judge people and you're always willing to lend a helping hand.

Set boundaries and be clear with them. Ask yourself why it happened. You let yourself become a victim of their manipulative strategies. One of the main reasons this occurs is because you didn't set boundaries with the person and relationship. Maybe you never thought you had to, or you didn't think about making them clear. You just felt that once wouldn't hurt anything. It's time to think about the relationship you want and that you deserve to be treated with respect and compassion. Establish boundaries for your future relationships and make them clear from the start. If someone doesn't follow your boundaries, let them know. If they still won't listen, keep your distance or let them go.

Prepare yourself for difficult emotions. You're going to feel some of the worst emotions you've ever had through your process. It helps to put yourself in the state of mind that you'll experience more than your regular break-up feelings. For instance, you'll be angry, sad, and grieve but you'll also have anxiety, paranoia, shame, and fear. This is part of the trauma of toxic relationships. It's nearly impossible for people to handle these alone so you want to be open to seeking counselling, talking to friends, and family.

Change your identity. It's common to feel that you lost yourself in a narcissistic relationship. You might remember the person you were before, look in the mirror now and not recognise yourself. They've taken your identity, but this doesn't mean you can't get it back. The key is to remember that you won't be the exact same person you were before. You've emotionally and psychologically grown. You're overcoming a challenging part in your life, and it will make you stronger. It will give you more motivation to succeed. Start talking to your highest self again and focus on developing your new identity.

*"It is our attitude at the beginning of a difficult task
which, more than anything else,
will affect its successful outcome."*
- William James (Picard, 2018)

Chapter 5:

Gratitude

By now you've heard this word, "gratitude." You've probably seen it many times in other books or articles. You've read several affirmations that help you focus on reaching your happiness and learning how to be grateful for what you have.

Gratitude is an expression of appreciation for yourself, other people, objects, and even what you don't have. It's often a spontaneous feeling. For example, you're visiting your grandparents' house and they hand you a bag of goodies to take home. Even if you expected it because it's part of their routine, you're still grateful for them and the treats. They thought about you, and you cherish the taste of the food because you know it won't be a part of your life forever.

Sometimes you need to reach for your attitude of gratitude. You need to use certain strategies, such as writing in a journal or telling someone "thank you" to feel the emotion. When you're struggling mentally, emotionally, or physically you can find yourself feeling better just by focusing on something you're grateful for, such as a home, family, or your talent. You might even take time during your day to think back on your life and be thankful for all the steps you've taken to get where you are today.

Most people think that you can only feel gratitude when you're happy and you perceive everything is going right. But, it's important to reach into your emotions and pull out your thankful thoughts, especially when you're struggling.

Be Grateful for Your Failures

C.S. Lewis wrote several astonishing novels like *The Lion, The Witch and The Wardrobe* but one of his greatest quotes is "Failures are finger posts on the road to achievement" (Edberg, 2016). What did Lewis mean when he sent these words out into the world? Do people like Lewis, Stephen King, William Shakespeare, and Charles

Dickens face failures like you do? Yes, they do and this is what Lewis wanted you to know. He wanted you to know that he faced failure just like all of his readers. He also wanted you to know that it's these failures that led him down his path of success.

It's easy to fall victim to the inner critic or pity voice inside of you when you feel rejected. You believe that you're the only one who is facing this failure. You question your abilities or wonder why you didn't work harder. You start dragging your feet down a dusty road and question if you'll ever reach your dreams. As you continue to slowly walk, you see your goals slip further away from your reach.

The next failure comes and it's even more devastating. Now, you're starting to fear failure. You worry every time you give your boss a completed project because you imagine the worst. You think about everything they'll find wrong with it and wish that you would've spent more time ensuring every detail was perfect.

It's time to let go of this mindset because, as you've heard before, nothing and no one is perfect. There is always something you can do to improve your personality, work, or how you treat someone else. This doesn't mean that you're not a good or worthy person. It means that you're always learning and focusing on your inner growth. When it comes to your failures or mistakes, one way to do this is through being grateful for them and accepting them as a learning opportunity. Of course, this is easier said than done but by following a series of steps you can overcome your failures.

1. **Don't take it personally**. You need to separate your identity and your failure. It's okay that you haven't found the right avenue to accomplish your task yet. It doesn't mean that you are a failure. There are many people who've had failures at the beginning of their career and become notable people who continue to have failures. For example, Jeff Bezos, the owner of Amazon, developed a phone only to pull the idea a few weeks after release because of all the negative feedback from his customers. He didn't take it as a failure, he took it as an opportunity to change course in the product.

2. **Don't dwell on your failure.** Like most people, you obsess over your failure because you want to know what went wrong. If you're taking it as a learning opportunity, look at what happened and then do what you can to change it next time but then move on. Don't go back to your failure and analyse your mistakes over and over. When you're focusing too heavily on the past you can't continue to shape your future.

3. **Look at it in a different way.** Take a step back and think about how you're looking at the situation. For example, you grew up in a household that gave you an unhealthy view of

failure. Your parents didn't see it as an opportunity for growth; they saw it as a moment of bad decisions or laziness. The belief you built around failure will give you the match to light the fire. You need to change your thought process and look at it in a different way. You can do this by thinking about what you would say to a friend or your child in the same situation. Focus on your compassionate voice when you're helping yourself through a mistake.

Benefits of Gratitude for Everlasting Peace and Happiness

It's easier to focus on the negative over the positive because your brain is wired that way. You feel that it's better to expect the worst-case scenario. It's easy to take your loved ones and friends for granted or to forget about your blessings in life. To transform your negative mindset into a positive one, you need to focus on ways to change your thought patterns. Without this step, you'll feel that you're stuck. It's like you keep turning the wheel but because of a broken connection, you're not going forward.

You might feel changing your thought process is a lot of work, but in reality, it focuses on one important step that will lead you down a path of everlasting happiness—gratitude. Once you start feeling grateful for every piece of your life, everything else will fall into place. But this isn't the only benefit of gratitude.

Another benefit is developing your relationship in a more positive light. You'll become more trusting of people, and they will feel that you're a person they can trust. Others will start to see you as someone who will talk to them when they call or believe in them, even when they feel like no one else does. This happens because you've become more thankful for the people around you and your relationships. It doesn't matter if they're a coworker that you communicate with in meetings or your significant other. You feel fortunate to have them in your life and you focus on treating them better. You'll start to tell them how much you appreciate them, which will strengthen your bond.

When you become grateful, you start destroying your negative thoughts. There is only so much room in your mind and body for your thoughts and energy. This means that in order to bring new energy you need to release some of your old energy. For example, when you meditate you focus on releasing your bad feelings every time you exhale. Then, when you inhale you imagine positive energy flowing in with your breath and throughout your body. You want to follow the same pattern with your thoughts but instead of meditating, you can simply change the direction of your thoughts through gratitude. For instance, when you think "I'm not understanding this because I'm dumb," change your thought to say, "I'm not understanding this, but that's okay because I will when it's explained in a different way."

You'll feel more productive during the day because you decrease your self-doubt and become more motivated to succeed. Furthermore, when you're grateful, you're in a better mood, which makes you want to keep busy with work or projects that you enjoy. Your self-esteem increases and you start to feel better about yourself mentally, giving you the ambition to challenge yourself. Once you know that you're capable of completing a project, you're more likely to follow through with your goals.

Gratitude will give you a stronger sense of peace because it limits the stress you feel. It doesn't matter if you're given another project to complete in a week or if you're laid off due to uncontrollable circumstances. You'll know that the best course of action is to take a deep breath and tell yourself, "everything will be okay in the end." When you feel calmer, you'll think more clearly and rationally. You'll fall asleep easier and stay asleep throughout the night. You'll also focus on eating healthier, exercising more, and taking better care of your overall health. It's truly amazing how gratitude can do so much for you. It will really give you happiness that will last a lifetime!

Simple Ways to Practise Gratitude

You know the benefits of gratitude. You know you want to create everlasting happiness in your life, but you're not sure how to do this. There are many options that you can follow when developing your grateful attitude.

1. **Watch the sunset or sunrise.** One way that you can experience the thankful mindset is to bring yourself out into nature and focus on the beauty of the sunrise or sunset. While you want to be careful not to stare directly into the sun and to protect your eyes, you also want to note the gorgeous colours that the sun, clouds, and sky make together as the sun rises and sets. Close your eyes and take in the warmth of the sun and acknowledge how it helps you start or end another wonderful day.
2. **Get yourself some flowers.** If you love flowers, you don't need to wait for your partner to give you some. Instead, go out and purchase your own flowers or pick them directly from nature. Go for a walk and pluck a few beautiful flowers that can help brighten your home, office, and life.

3. **Smile at a stranger.** Go back to a time when you were having a bad day or moment and someone smiled at you. Maybe you walked into your home after a long day and your partner or children gave you a smile. Maybe it was a stranger as you walked down the street. Think back to this time and how it helped change your mood from negative to positive. Did you know that you can get the same feeling when you smile at a stranger? The next time you need a little boost of gratitude, take time to look at someone you meet walking down the street or in a store and give them a smile. Notice how your mood changes and how you start to feel that you start to get a little pep in your step.
4. **Say "Thank you."** You don't need to wait for someone to give you something or tell you a compliment to say, "thank you." You can say these two words any time of the day, especially when you're feeling a little down and finding yourself emotionally or mentally struggling. Simply close your eyes, take a deep breath, and say "thank you." You can say it mentally or out loud. You can imagine saying it to the universe for everything they've given you or to yourself for working hard.
5. **Write in a journal.** You don't need to take time every day to write in a gratitude journal, but you

should follow this process a few times a week. You can write about anything you want, but you want to end on a happy note. For example, you can discuss your day, the challenges you faced, and how you overcame them. You can write about people and why you appreciate them, what makes you grateful about your work, or anything else. You can also focus on one prompt every day. For instance, one day you might talk about your blessings within your family and the next time within your job. You can also write down three silly things your children did that day, what you could thank someone for, about a time someone did something for you and why you're grateful for it, or three possessions you would hold on to if you had to sell everything else and why you choose them.

6. **Take time to read and learn.** You don't need to go back to school but if there is something you want to learn more about, start looking into it. For example, if you want to learn how to crochet, check out a couple of beginner books or find a local group that will help develop your skills. You can also focus on reading a new book every week or one a month on a different topic to help broaden your knowledge.

One of the main ways to practise gratitude is to simply be thankful for your experiences in your life, even your struggles. The key is to find ways that resonate with you. For instance, if you enjoy nature, you'll find the beauty in nature and ways to be thankful quickly. If you're a social butterfly, focus on spending time with your friends, family, and others. However, you also need to take time for yourself because a grateful attitude starts with you.

You Are Never Alone

One of the biggest challenges in life, especially emotionally, is the belief that you're going through your struggles alone. This makes you feel like you need to suffer alone. You worry that reaching out for help means that people won't care, understand, or they'll see you as a burden.

When you practise gratitude, you slowly start to realise that no matter what is happening to you—you're not alone. You have family and friends who support you and want to see you succeed. You have colleagues who will lend a shoulder. You also realise there are thousands, if not millions, of people who know what you're going through because they've gone or are going through it. The challenge of walking through any door in your life becomes easier. You start to feel that you can take on the world and anything you're facing.

Once you reach this point in your soul, you become more grateful. You are thankful for everyone who is around you and how they've helped you grow. Even if they hurt you in the past, you praise them for the lessons they've taught you.

Tips for Keeping a Gratitude Journal

What are you grateful about at this moment? If you want, take a moment to write it down. Are you thankful for your family, career, or having a home? Pause everything and focus on your first thought and think about what you would write about it.

Now, focus on your mood. Do you feel happier, lighter, or more positive? Imagine waking up and starting your day with the same feeling. Instead of mentally playing all of your problems and what you need to do that day, you can focus on your gratitude. You can take time a few days a week or every morning to ensure you think positively before anything else. All you need is a few minutes in the morning to help you get out of bed and get ready for the day.

The biggest challenge with keeping a journal is following through. It takes time to establish a habit or change your routine, even the slightest bit. For instance, if you're used to sleeping in until the last minute, you will feel too rushed to take five minutes to write down your thankful thought. If you struggle getting started, use steps to help yourself adjust to allowing that time. Start by waking up five minutes earlier and then simply lie there awake. A few days later, you can wake up and get up. Once you're comfortable waking up earlier, pick up the journal and start writing.

To help you keep with the rhythm of writing, follow these tips.

Connect with something or someone specific. Even when you're feeling generally grateful for your life, you want to zoom in on one topic. You should write in as much detail as possible because you'll connect with your emotions easier. If you're having trouble focusing, look at your surroundings. Why did you purchase the object sitting to your left? Or, pick the last book you read that you absolutely loved. What was it about the book that makes you happy?

Buy a journal. There are many types of gratitude journals that you can purchase. Some of them will have quotes while others will have prompts to get your thoughts moving. But, you can always choose a regular journal with a beautiful cover that you adore. Pick one that speaks to you.

Your emotions are more important. You should write down everything that you feel necessary, but don't let this get in the way of what you feel. Research shows that it's not the writing that keeps you going, it's the connections to your emotions. Many journalists will stop writing over time because they feel they're repetitive and just going through the motions. They don't believe that it's helping them feel happier and more thankful. The main reasons this can happen is because they don't include their emotions in their writing, so they start to treat journaling as a task instead of a lifestyle choice.

Don't overdo it. You might enjoy writing every morning, but the majority of people say it's more beneficial to pick two to three days a week to write. You need to find the best solution for yourself so you can truly feel grateful.

Why You Should Be Thankful for What You Don't Have

When you start bringing more gratitude into your life, it's easy to focus on what you have. You think about your family, friends, work, hobbies, talents, skills, pets, house, and so much more. While this is a great step in the right direction, you don't want to leave out what you lack.

That's right, it's important to take time to say "thank you" for what you don't have in your life, even if you really want it.

You are probably asking yourself, "Why should I be thankful for what I don't have?" Well, here are a few good reasons.

It tames your jealousy. The neighbours bought another new car. Your coworker received the promotion. Your friend got better grades than you. Your sibling has a better paying job. There are a lot of bits and pieces in your life that can make you jealous. It's not that you don't want to see other people successful; you just don't want to be left out. You want the same type of success or even more. It's not a feeling you should be ashamed of because it's a natural reaction. That said, you also want to keep your jealousy in control, and taking time to say,

"Thank you for not giving me that promotion," can help keep it in place.

It keeps you motivated. Just because you don't have what you want now doesn't mean you can't have it someday. Take a moment to reflect on your goals and note what you can do to make your wishes come true. You can have anything you want in the world, but the only way you'll reach it is by working toward it.

It teaches delayed gratification. It's nice to hear about people who land their dream job right away, but what about the one who climbed slowly up the ladder? Their story is just as important. In fact, it's usually more inspiring for other people. Often, reaching your goals requires patience and dedication. These are characteristics that aren't always easy to focus on, especially when you see people sprinting ahead of you. When you're starting to feel frustrated because you see yourself as left in the dust, take a moment to be grateful for your path in life. No matter what you're waiting for, it helps you learn about delayed gratification. Your time will come; it'll just take a bit longer.

You realise that you have enough. When you get into the mindset that you need or want something, you start to forget about what you have. You might start to think everything you have isn't good enough. This can lead you to thinking that you're not good enough, which can cause you to struggle with anxiety and depression. When you're thankful for what you don't have, you realise you have everything you need.

A Dozen Ways to Love Your Body

How many times a day do you look in the mirror and notice your flaws? Do you ever find yourself scanning over your body slowly to look for something that is physically wrong, such as a zit, damaged hair, or eyes that are too far apart? Now, think of how many times you point out the parts of your body that you love. Do you realise a difference in your thought process? If so, don't feel bad because you're not alone. Most people pick out their flaws before they talk about the love they have for your body.

But, it's time to change this with these dozen ways to love your body.

1. Speak kindly to yourself every morning. You should do this throughout the day, and work to stop yourself from saying anything negative, but it's more important in the morning because it sets how you'll feel about yourself for the rest of the day.
2. Eat food that is healthy for your body and mind. The old saying "you are what you eat" is true. When you eat unhealthy foods, you feel poorly about yourself. You're more likely to suffer from depression, anxiety, and other mental illnesses.

It's also easier to get sick from viruses and bacteria.

3. Don't just smile at other people, smile at your reflection! Go on, show yourself your sparkling smile.
4. Dress in a way that makes you feel confident. If you feel lazy and dirty in your pyjamas because you slept in them, don't continue wearing them throughout the day, even if you're lounging. Wash your face and put on different clothes. Even if they're Yoga pants and a t-shirt, you'll feel better.
5. Be patient with yourself. You're a human who will make mistakes and still has a lot of life lessons to learn.
6. Remind yourself that your body is just a shell. What matters is who you are on the inside.
7. Teach yourself not to be ashamed of your flaws because they're parts of your character. Be proud of who you are and remember no one is perfect.
8. Take time to not only focus on improving yourself but to also be grateful for where you are in life and who you've become.
9. Recognise that eating healthily and taking care of yourself is part of keeping your mind and body healthy. It's not meant to be a chore.
10. Never be afraid to start over. If you want to improve a piece of your life, set a date for when

you'll start. Don't wake up in the morning and tell yourself, "Today, I'm going to start eating better." Instead say, "I will start my diet on Thursday next week." If you find that you give in to your cravings and stray away from your diet, be gentle with yourself and go back to focusing on your plan.

11. Understand that you will have bad days where you just can't find the beauty in your body. Tell yourself that it's okay to feel this way. The key is to take it one day at a time. Remember, tomorrow will be a better day.
12. Lather your body with lotion, cocoa butter, or soap. Take time to smell the aroma and notice the feeling you get from moisturised skin.

A 30-Day Gratitude Challenge

You've probably heard of a gratitude challenge. They last several days and are known to help you get into a grateful mindset. They're popular because many people don't consider themselves naturally thankful, which isn't true. Everyone has the ability inside of them, the key is learning how to bring it out through practice—which is exactly what a challenge does.

These are difficult challenges, so there's no need to be afraid. Furthermore, you don't go into competition with anyone but yourself. You fulfil the requirements by doing what the challenge tells you to do every day. You can make it fun by using it as a team building exercises at work, with friends, or family.

It's helpful to start a journal during this time where you focus on the activity you complete. You can write about any struggles you had, how it made you feel, and anything else that pops into your mind along the way.

Day 1: Write down three positive ways to describe yourself and then place them where you can read them every day.

Day 2: Text someone with an explanation of why you're grateful for them.

Day 3: When you feel frustrated because something isn't going right, think of something that is going well.

Day 4: Write down one thing that you're grateful for.

Day 5: Call someone and explain to them why you're grateful for them.

Day 6: Write a letter to your future self and discuss five ways to be grateful for your life. Put this letter somewhere safe for you to read it whenever you need a boost.

Day 7: Name your alarm in a positive way, such as "You're going to have a great day!"

Day 8: What two abilities are you grateful for?

Day 9: What moment this week are you thankful about? Write it down and put it up so you can see it. You can also repeat this process every week by writing down a new grateful moment.

Day 10: What season brings out the more gratitude in you?

Day 11: Write a letter to someone you're grateful for and then call them to see when you can stop by for a visit.

When you go there, read the letter to them so they know what they mean to you.

Day 12: What place are you thankful for today?

Day 13: Write down all of your accomplishments and then find a way to thank yourself for working hard and staying motivated.

Day 14: Think about two memories that make you feel happy. Write them down and keep them somewhere you can see them easily.

Day 15: Take time to analyse what needs are being met for you in your life and say, "thank you."

Day 16: Write down one thing that you believe you're good at.

Day 17: Find a location in your community where you can volunteer. Contact the organization and talk to them about their opportunities and set up a time to help them with a project.

Day 18: Offer to hug someone that you're grateful for.

Day 19: Find someone that you're thankful for and invite them out for lunch.

Day 20: Take time to reflect about something that you lack and say "thank you" for not having it at this moment.

Day 21: Think of someone who could use some extra appreciation and thank them for everything they do for you.

Day 22: Go for a walk and take a picture of something in nature you find beautiful.

Day 23: Reflect on how much your gratitude mindset has changed since you started this challenge.

Day 24: Think about one of your favourite gratitude challenges so far and repeat it today.

Day 25: Talk to someone who you're grateful for and explain this challenge. Ask them if they would be interested in starting their own and help them get started, if they agree.

Day 26: Write down everything you remember eating today and be thankful for the food. Don't judge whether it was "bad" or "good" just say "thank you."

Day 27: Think about someone that has helped you grow as a person and contact them. Tell them how much they mean to you and what they did for you.

Day 28: Do something unexpected for someone today.

Day 29: Take time to notice all of the devices (cell phone, computer, iPad, etc.) that have helped you today and say, "thank you."

Day 30: Take a few minutes and reflect about how you feel after participating in this challenge. Write it down and then challenge yourself to keep your gratitude mindset going for the rest of the year.

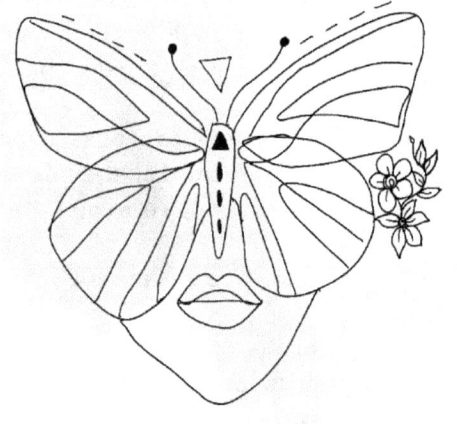

Conclusion

Before you read any further into this conclusion, I want you to sit back and think about how you felt before you started this book. Close your eyes and try to reach into your memory of emotions. Think back to what you were going through and why you chose this book. Now, ask yourself what has changed. Even if you don't feel a lot of difference yet, what do you notice is starting to change? Maybe you've started a gratitude journal or you're focusing on changing your negative thoughts into positive ones. You might be working on the 30-day gratitude challenge and finding that this is what you've needed in your life. You might also be learning how to control your negative emotions, so they don't control you.

Through these pages, we went on a journey together. You learned more about yourself, your emotions, and your thoughts. You realised certain puzzle pieces of your life have fallen on the ground and you're slowly picking them up and placing them back where they belong. You now understand that to reach your full potential you need to face your fears and talk to your highest self. You've gained knowledge and understand strategies that can help you overcome challenges, cope, and grow.

This book has helped you learn some of the most powerful tools for your life so you can focus on the most important person—*you*. Don't be afraid or ashamed to be who you are. There is no one like you. You have a passion within you that only you can bring out into the world. You have a purpose. Reach into the depths of your soul, so you can fulfil your mission.

Be proud of yourself for what you have accomplished. I know that I'm proud of you.

References

15 personal development quotes to help you invest in yourself. (2017). Success. https://www.success.com/15-personal-development-quotes-to-help-you-invest-in-yourself/

21 days of gratitude challenge. (n.d.). Www.Heart.Org. Retrieved June 16, 2020, from https://www.heart.org/en/healthy-living/healthy-lifestyle/mental-health-and-wellbeing/21-days-of-gratitude-infographic

Abrams, A. (2017). *8 steps to improving your self-esteem.* Psychology Today. https://www.psychologytoday.com/us/blog/nurturing-self-compassion/201703/8-steps-improving-your-self-esteem

Amatenstein, S. (2017, March 27). *How to overcome your fears, get unstuck, and fuel your success |...* Brian Tracy's Self Improvement & Professional Development Blog. https://www.briantracy.com/blog/personal-success/fight-or-flight-overcoming-your-fears/

Anxiety and Depression Association of America. (n.d.). *Facts & statistics.* Adaa.Org. https://adaa.org/about-adaa/press-room/facts-statistics#:~:text=Anxiety%20disorders%20are%20the%20most

Anxiety and Depression Association of America. (2019). *Tips*. Adaa.Org. https://adaa.org/tips

Barns, L. (2014, September). *Top 10 benefits of A good night's sleep*. The Sleep Matters Club; The Sleep Matters Club. https://www.dreams.co.uk/sleep-matters-club/top-10-benefits-good-nights-sleep/

Bellows, A. (2016, May 17). *Too tense? Tips for tackling the stress*. Psychcentral.Com. https://psychcentral.com/lib/too-tense-tips-for-tackling-the-stress/

Berry smoothie bowl | minimalist baker recipes. (2016, August 5). Minimalist Baker. https://minimalistbaker.com/favorite-smoothie-bowl-5-minutes/

Borresen, K. (2018, March 5). *11 subtle signs you might be in an emotionally abusive relationship*. HuffPost Canada; HuffPost Canada. https://www.huffpost.com/entry/signs-of-emotional-abuse-relationship_n_5a999fbee4b0a0ba4ad31a4d

Bressert, S. (2016, May 17). *The impact of stress.* Psych Central. https://psychcentral.com/lib/the-impact-of-stress/

Burgess, L. (2017, October 7). *8 benefits of crying: Why do we cry, and when to seek support.* Www.Medicalnewstoday.Com. https://www.medicalnewstoday.com/articles/319631#benefits-of-crying

Edberg, H. (2016, February 25). *How to overcome failure: 9 powerful habits.* Positivityblog.Com. https://www.positivityblog.com/how-to-overcome-failure/

Edberg, H. (2018, January 10). *13 powerful ways to overcome self-doubt (so you can finally move forward in life).* Positivityblog.Com. https://www.positivityblog.com/overcome-self-doubt/

Exploring Your Mind. (2016, October 30). *Personal growth to strengthen your self-esteem.* Exploring Your Mind. https://exploringyourmind.com/personal-growth-strengthen-self-esteem/#:~:text=The%20way%20you%20view%20yourself

Fox, A. (2017, May 18). *10 expert-approved ways to turn around a crappy day.* HuffPost.

https://www.huffpost.com/entry/bad-day-tips_n_59122641e4b0a58297e0492e

Gunter, P. (2019, August 9). *The power of positive thinking: 7 mindful habits for creating positive thoughts.* The Law Of Attraction. https://www.thelawofattraction.com/power-of-positive-thinking/#:~:text=When%20you%20practice%20positive%20thinking

Hays, J. (2014, August 12). *30 ways to practice self-love and be good to yourself.* Lifehack. https://www.lifehack.org/articles/communication/30-ways-practice-self-love-and-good-yourself.html#:~:text=Start%20each%20day%20by%20telling%20yourself%20something%20really%20positive.&text=Surround%20yourself%20with%20people%20who

Health Navigator. (2019). *Anxiety.* Health Navigator New Zealand. https://www.healthnavigator.org.nz/health-a-z/a/anxiety/

Hughes, A. (2015). A 5-step guide to cultivating a relationship with your higher self. DOYOU.COM. https://www.doyou.com/a-five-step-guide-to-cultivating-a-relationship-with-your-higher-self-33411/

Iliopoulos, A. (2017, August 30). *Developing self awareness – the 5 stages of awareness mastery.* The

Quintessential Mind. https://thequintessentialmind.com/developing-self-awareness/

Kohr, A. (2015, May 12). *10 simple ways to practice self-care (it's easier than you think)*. Wanderlust. https://wanderlust.com/journal/simple-ways-practice-self-care/

Mackay, H. (2020). *We need to learn how to move on from mistakes*. Bizjournals.Com. https://www.bizjournals.com/bizjournals/how-to/growth-strategies/2020/02/we-need-to-learn-how-to-move-on-from-mistakes.html

Manson, M. (n.d.). *5 skills to help you develop emotional intelligence*. Mark Manson. https://markmanson.net/emotions/emotional-intelligence-skills

Marsh, J. (2011). *Tips for keeping a gratitude journal*. Greater Good. https://greatergood.berkeley.edu/article/item/tips_for_keeping_a_gratitude_journal

Mcleod, S. (2020). *Maslow's hierarchy of needs*. Simply Psychology. https://www.simplypsychology.org/maslow.html#:~:text=Maslow

Megan. (2018, May 22). *30-Day gratitude challenge to jump start your new lifestyle*. Page Flutter.

https://pageflutter.com/30-day-gratitude-challenge/

Nelson, J. (2020, June 10). *30 signs your self-confidence is dangerously low and you need to learn to love yourself.* Thought Catalog. https://thoughtcatalog.com/january-nelson/2020/06/30-signs-your-self-confidence-is-dangerously-low-and-you-need-to-learn-to-love-yourself/

Newsonen, S. (2015, May 20). *3 reasons why you have to trust your gut.* Psychology Today. https://www.psychologytoday.com/us/blog/the-path-passionate-happiness/201505/3-reasons-why-you-have-trust-your-gut

Njoki, L. (2020, June 8). *8 amazing ways you'll change when you start to put yourself first.* Thought Catalog. https://thoughtcatalog.com/leah-njoki/2020/06/8-amazing-ways-youll-change-when-you-start-to-put-yourself-first/

Oldham, P. (2020). *How to release yourself from your past.* Simplemindfulness.Com. https://www.simplemindfulness.com/release-from-your-past/

One you. (2019). Www.Nhs.Uk. https://www.nhs.uk/oneyou/every-mind-matters/top-tips-to-improve-your-mental-wellbeing/

Picard, C. (2018, January 8). *41 inspirational quotes for when your mood could use a boost.* Good Housekeeping; Good Housekeeping. https://www.goodhousekeeping.com/health/wellness/g2401/inspirational-quotes/

Pietrangelo, A., & Watson, S. (2017, March 29). *The effects of stress on your body.* Healthline. https://www.healthline.com/health/stress/effects-on-body#1

Raypole, C. (2020, March 30). *Recovery from narcissistic abuse is possible — here's how.* Healthline. https://www.healthline.com/health/mental-health/9-tips-for-narcissistic-abuse-recovery#identity

Riordan, H. (2019, January 25). *12 benefits of gratitude that will bring you everlasting happiness.* Thought Catalog. https://thoughtcatalog.com/holly-riordan/2019/01/benefits-of-gratitude/

Rogers, S. (2017, November 16). *5 tips for failing forward.* Inc.Com. https://www.inc.com/entrepreneurs-organization/forward-ever-backward-never.html

Roy, S. (2014, July 14). *7 mindfulness steps: A quick and easy guide*. Happiness India Project; Sandip Roy. https://happyproject.in/mindfulness-7-steps/

Sanders, L. (2016, September 8). *28 simple ways to practice gratitude*. Thought Catalog. https://thoughtcatalog.com/leena-sanders/2016/09/28-simple-ways-to-practice-gratitude/

Seale, Q. (2019). *Amazing quotes about being yourself*. Keepinspiring.Me. https://www.keepinspiring.me/quotes-about-being-yourself/

Spahic, M. (2018, April 4). *How to maintain a healthy eating lifestyle*. USPM. https://www.uspm.com/how-to-maintain-a-healthy-eating-lifestyle/

Tartakovsky, M. (2016, May 17). *Therapists spill: 12 ways to accept yourself*. Psychcentral.Com. https://psychcentral.com/lib/therapists-spill-12-ways-to-accept-yourself/

Ways to look after your mental health and wellbeing. (2017). Think Mental Health. https://www.thinkmentalhealthwa.com.au/abo

ut-mental-health-wellbeing/ways-to-look-after-your-mental-health/

Williams, A. (2020a, January 21). *6 ways to take charge of your fear and anxiety.* Thought Catalog. https://thoughtcatalog.com/amy-reis-williams/2020/01/6-ways-to-take-charge-of-your-fear-and-anxiety/

Williams, A. (2020b, March 6). *Use your pain as A catalyst for growth.* Thought Catalog. https://thoughtcatalog.com/amy-reis-williams/2020/03/use-your-pain-as-a-catalyst-for-growth/

Woodbury, D. (2013, March 4). *10 little moments to practice mindful awareness.* HuffPost. https://www.huffpost.com/entry/mindfulness-practices_b_2790429

Wright, R. (2015, December 7). *4 reasons to be thankful for what you don't have this holiday season.* The Odyssey Online. https://www.theodysseyonline.com/4-reasons-thankful-for-what-you-dont-have

www.ingramcontent.com/pod-product-compliance
Lightning Source LLC
Chambersburg PA
CBHW051400290426
44108CB00015B/2096